By providing his readers with an engaging personal and pastoral reflection on the problem of Evil and the biblical doctrine of the Devil, Dr. Lomax charts a course out of the fog of Sin and the Fall into the sunlight of living abundant, peaceful and fulfilling lives. Dr. Lomax earns my endorsement for the way he brings biblical and theological expression to his experiences from the neighborhood rivalries of his early years to his mature ministry with individuals, families and communities on the front lines of confronting violence and death.
Dr. Jeffrey S. Rogers, Senior Minister, First Baptist Church, Greenville, S.C.

This book written By Rev. Doctor Stephen S. Lomax is easily readable and understandable. It is supported excellently by Biblical passages. Readers will find it very pleasurably to read. It is written with great thought and scholar. Bible students will find it very helpful in studying different areas of the Bible, particularly the area dealing with the Devil. I recommend this book as a good supplementary resource for students of the Bible. It was written with much time and research to make it plain and helpful.
Doctor S. C. Cureton, Pastor of the Reedy River Baptist Church and Past President of the National Baptist Convention, U. S. A., Inc.

Congratulations to the Reverend Doctor Stephen S. Lomax for the writing of this book. It is well grounded in Biblical facts. This book both calls the Christian to attention and sends a strong clarion call and warning to the unsaved. Reading it will make you wiser and believing the words of it will help you find salvation and peace of mind.
Doctor J. Willie Henderson, Pastor of the Tree of Life Baptist Church and former First Vice President at Large of the National Congress of Christian Education, U. S. A., Inc.

Every individual on planted earth has a very real enemy. He is intelligent; he is cunning and is determined to derail every person's life. That enemy is the devil.
Doctor Stephen Lomax has provided an excellent work in describing our enemy and his relationship to the behavior of us all. In addition, he has provided us with clear insights to defend ourselves against our common enemy. And has shown us how to escape "the wiles of the

devil." I would encourage anyone who has struggled with the good and evil in his life to read Dr. Lomax's book

Michael W. Bearden, Pastor of the First Baptist Church of Fountain Inn, S. C.

This is a splendid, in-depth evaluation of the reality of the devil and his mode of operations in the earth. Dr. Lomax does a magnificent job of explaining the original purpose and plan of God for man which, by the way, is the gospel of the Kingdom of God. He also explains how God's original intentions for man become thwarted and distorted because of our innate capacity to be influenced and manipulated by the evil one, Satan. This corruption is responsible for the overwhelming majority of the suffering, violence, evil, and destruction we experience in the human family, and this is what God through Christ came to deliver us from. Thank you, Dr. Lomax, for helping to open our blinded minds.

Pastor Curtis Johnson; Valley Brook Outreach Baptist Church, Pelzer, SC

This compelling new study on this age-old topic sheds a bright light on what we need to know when dealing with today's troubled world. The church especially can gain much insight into the "personification" of the DEVIL.

A must read for progressive pastors.

Rev. Guy E. Sullivan; Pastor of the Good Hope Baptist Church, Waterloo, S. C.

DR. S.S. LOMAX:

YOU ARE TO BE COMMENDED, FOR SUCH A VERY TIMELY WORK ON THE SUBJECT OF DEMONOLOGY, THIS BOOK WILL BE VERY HELPFUL TO THE BELIEVER THAT'S READY FOR SPIRITUAL WARFARE.

THANKS FOR EXPOSING SATAN AND HIS DEMONS. II COR. 2:11 "LEST SATAN SHOULD GET AN ADVANTAGE OF US: FOR WE ARE NOT IGNORANT OF HIS DEVICES."

TERRY A. KING, PASTOR OF THE ROCK OF AGES BAPTIST CHURCH, GREENVILLE, S.C.

Did The Devil Makes Me Do It; forces one to examine the origin and existence of the devil and more importantly God and their respective roles in our personal and societal behavior. I was impressed by the discussion regarding the absence of a biblical origin for the ravages of racism. This book makes one evaluate the human fragilities of blame, suffering, lack of personal responsibility, societal clinging to divisive behavior, ineffective childrearing; and the absence of spirituality and possessing a church foundation. It is a good manual for productive living and making the right choices with Biblical support. It is written in a conversational tone.
I highly recommend it if you really want to know **why we do what we do**!
Clyde E. Henderson, MD; Cincinnati, Ohio

This timely exposition of the ways and means of the churches chief nemesis, Satan, brings the believer face-to-face with the wiles of the devil referenced in the Holy Scriptures. This work will stand for ages to come as a source for understanding what it means to wrestle not against flesh and blood, but against principalities, against powers, against the rulers of this world and against spiritual wickedness in high places. Through his succinct description of the work of the enemy and the comprehensive battle plan laid out in this book, the novice as well as the seasoned believer can find the encouragement to resist and defeat the devil. Dr. Lomax has taken a question that has been pondered through the years and brought clarity, understanding, and a single answer.
Elder W. Scott Hunter, Upper Room Church of God in Christ; Raleigh, N.C. & Chief of Police.

Dr. Lomax provides highly insightful information about the cunning and destructive acts of satan. He explains how and why Christians today should overcome the works of the most dangerous hinderance to the abundant life God designed. In these last days we cannot afford to be ignorant of this important topic. Dr. Lomax's work is timely and truly eye-opening.
Pamela G. Wilson, author of *Finding Soul Brothers*.

DID THE DEVIL MAKE ME DO IT?

DR. STEPHEN S. LOMAX

authorHOUSE®

AuthorHouse™
1663 Liberty Drive, Suite 200
Bloomington, IN 47403
www.authorhouse.com
Phone: 1-800-839-8640

© 2008 Dr. Stephen S. Lomax. All rights reserved.

No part of this book may be reproduced, stored in a retrieval system, or transmitted by any means without the written permission of the author.

First published by AuthorHouse 8/25/2008

ISBN: 978-1-4389-1369-8 (sc)
ISBN: 978-1-4389-1371-1 (hc)

Library of Congress Control Number: 2008907912

Printed in the United States of America
Bloomington, Indiana

This book is printed on acid-free paper.

ACKNOWLEDGEMENTS

I must acknowledge God, the Father, God the Son and God, the Holy Spirit for the inspiration, courage, confidence and knowledge to write the book. If it had not been for the Lord, Lord I don't know what I would do!

I thank God for the love, support and longevity of Mrs. Frances Delores Shaw Lomax. Your love and spiritual leadership has been superior down through the 35 years of marriage. May God richly bless you; if it had not been for you, I don't know what I would do? Thanks so much from the depths of my heart and soul.

To my children, Africa, Kenya; Stephanie and Jerrell, I love you with agape (unlimited and non expectant) love. Over the years, you have brought so much pride and joy to me that all of the money at Fort Knox could not buy. Love ya all!

To my two sons in law (Todd and Jaron), you have added much to the Lomax family and I am proud to call you sons. Keep up the good work.

To my grand children, Stephen Samuel Lomax, II (Nuke) and Zhain Mackenzie Roux, if I had only known what emotions you would bring to my heart, I would have had you first. I can not put into words, what deep love and joy that I feel just looking at you. Stay close so that I can see you regularly.

To all of my brothers, Robert; James Willie, and Joe Louis and my one remaining sister, Judy and her husband, James (Boot); thank you so much for the defense and support over the years. It meant and still means much.

To all of the members of the New Life in Christ Missionary Baptist Church, words can not describe or express the love and admiration that I have for you. We are family and God and I will never forget your commitment to righteousness. May heaven continue to smile upon you; I know I will.

Special thanks to those of you that assisted me in the editing process of the book and for your much needed commentary: Mrs. Alberta Hunter, great job; Mrs. Essie Sullivan superb comments; Ms. Mary Williams; just wonderful. A gold medal to Ms. Carol Cook for the tireless gift of time and encouraging support to the project. I am forever grateful.

Also I must thank Reverend James Clark; Reverend Terry King; Reverend Tony Boyce; Mr. James Mckie; Mr. Anthony Bennon; Mr. Carlton Manley; Ms. Tammie Shaw; Mrs. Pam Wilson; Ms. Ahjia Sullivan and the Mitch Smith family, plus a host of other family and friends.

Much appreciation to the endorsers of the book; I could not have succeeded without you.

CONTENTS

FOUNDATIONAL SCRIPTURES	XI
CHAPTER I	1
PRELUDE AND PURPOSE!	
CHAPTER II	12
THE DEVIL AND EVIL: TWO PEAS IN A POD!	
AN ASSESSMENT OF EVIL AND ITS SOURCE!	
CHAPTER III	27
A WORD ABOUT THE THEME!	
A TRIP DOWN MEMORY LANE	
CHAPTER IV	43
WHO IS THE DEVIL?	
PERSONAL PERCEPTIONS OF THE DEVIL!	
CHAPTER V	54
WHO REALLY IS THE DEVIL?	
THE BIBLICAL REALITIES OF THE DEVIL!	
CHAPTER VI	77
DOES GOD MAKE ME DO WHAT I DO? WHO IS GOD?	
PERSONAL AND BIBLICAL REALITIES OF GOD	
CHAPTER VII	98
WHO IS MAN?	
CHAPTER VIII	113
WHY I REALLY DO WHAT I DO?	

CHAPTER IX   133
WHY DO THE RIGHTEOUS SUFFER?
SOME GOOD PEOPLE IN SOME BAD SITUATIONS!

CHAPTER X   154
HELPFUL HINTS ON HOW TO DEFEAT THE DEVIL!

CHAPTER XI   165
HELPFUL HINTS ON HOW TO BE BLESSED BY GOD!
"OBEDIENCE IS BETTER THAN SACRIFICE!" "WHEN PRAISES
GO UP; BLESSINGS COME DOWN!"

CHAPTER XII   179
A FINAL THOUGHT!
**IF YOU DON'T KNOW WHO YOU'RE MESSING
WITH, YOU NEED TO ASK SOMEBODY!**

END NOTES ON BOOK: 191

FOUNDATIONAL SCRIPTURES

"Now the serpent was more crafty than any of the wild animals the LORD God had made. He said to the woman, "Did God really say, 'You must not eat from any tree in the garden'?" The woman said to the serpent, "We may eat fruit from the trees in the garden, but God did say, 'You must not eat fruit from the tree that is in the middle of the garden, and you must not touch it, or you will die.' You will not surely die," the serpent said to the woman. For God knows that when you eat of it, your eyes will be opened, and you will be like God; knowing good and evil.

When the woman saw that the fruit of the tree was good for food and pleasing to the eye, and also desirable for gaining wisdom, she took some and ate it. She also gave some to her husband, who was with her, and he ate it" (Gen. 3: 1-6 NIV).

"One day the angels came to present themselves before the Lord, and Satan also came with them. The Lord said to Satan, "Where have you come from?" Satan answered the Lord, "From roaming through the earth and going back and forth in it. Then the Lord said to Satan, "Have you considered my servant Job? There is no one on earth like him; he is blameless and upright, a man who fears God and shuns evil."

Does Job fear God for nothing?" Satan replied. Have you not put a hedge around him and his household and everything he has? You have blessed the work of his hands, so that his flocks and herds are spread throughout the land. But stretch out your hand and strike everything he has, and he will surely curse you to your face."

The Lord said to Satan, "Very well, then, everything he has is in your hands, but on the man himself do not lay a finger." Then Satan went out from the presence of the Lord" (Job 1: 6-12 NIV).

"Be sober; be vigilant; because your adversary, the devil, as a roaring lion, walketh about seeking whom he may devour: Whom resist stedfast in the faith, knowing that the same afflictions are accomplished in your brethren that are in the world. But the God of all grace, who hath called us unto his eternal glory by Christ Jesus, after that ye have suffered a while, make you perfect, stablish, strengthen, settled you" (I Peter 5: 8-10 KJV).

"For what I am doing, I do not understand. For what I will to do, that I do not practice; but what I hate, that I do. If then, I do what I will not to do, I agree with the law that it is good. But it is no longer I who do it, but sin that dwells in me. For I know that in me (that is, in my flesh), dwells nothing good; for the will is present with me, but how to perform what is good I do not find. For the good that I will to do, I do not do; but the evil that I will not to do, that I practice. Now if I do what I will not to do, it is no longer I who do it, but sin that dwells in me" (Romans 7: 15-20 NIV).

"But I see another law in my members, warring against the law of my mind, and bringing me into captivity to the law of sin which is in my members. O wretched man I am! Who will deliver me from this body of death? I thank God through Jesus Christ our Lord! So then, with the mind I myself serve the law of God, but with the flesh the law of sin" (Romans 7: 23-25 NIV)

WHY DID I DO THAT?

CHAPTER I
PRELUDE AND PURPOSE!

"God blessed them and said to them, "Be fruitful and increase in number; fill the earth and subdue it. Rule over the fish of the sea and the birds of the air and over every living creature that moves on the ground. Then God said, "I give you every seed-bearing plant on the face of the whole earth and every tree that has fruit with seed in it. They will be yours for food.

And to all the beasts of the earth and all the birds of the air and all the creatures that move on the ground, everything that has the breath of life in it, I give every green plant for food: And it was so" **(Gen. 1: 28-30 NIV).**

There are many books written today informing men and women of their purpose in life. There are just as many books written reminding them that God created them to be like Christ and live purposeful and blessed lives to the glory of God (<u>The Purpose Driven Life</u> by Rick Warren is one of the many).

Yet, having said that, a question of necessity arises: If indeed man was created and designed to live purposeful and blessed lives, what happened to change his outlook? It's obvious that a change has taken place, so what happened? Why are there so many miserable people in the world? Why are there so many stories of human tragedy, disaster and even suicide?

Briefly consider this: In the city of Greenville, South Carolina, one Saturday morning when I was a young man. There were two young men that I knew that said good-by to their wives and young children. As usual, they and some other young men went off to fellowship together. It was their custom on Saturday mornings.

However this particular Saturday, the two young men in question were running low on cash, so they co-sponsored a bottle of "Ripple." They debated briefly over which one of them would drink first. It was decided; and one of them turned the bottle up and drank practically all of the wine.

The other man stood in silence for a moment, astonished and finally angry. He pulled a gun out of his pocket and shot the other young man in the head, leaving him dead as a door-nail.

In the final analysis, one of the young men lay dead and the other would never again see the daylight out side of a prison cell. Additionally, there were two wives without husbands and children without fathers: A real American tragedy. Although it occurred about forty years ago, I will never forget the horror of watching the event unfold.

The question must be asked, again, "Why do these tragedies happen? And why in the world are there so many evil people heading for destruction? For more examples of tragedy, see chapter I, "The Devil and evil: Two Peas in a Pod."

Concerning the question of man's mass destruction, there can be no denial. Jesus said, "Enter through the narrow gate. For wide is the gate and broad is the road that leads to destruction, and many enter through it. But small is the gate and narrow the road that leads to life, and only a few find it" (Matthew 7: 13-14 NIV).

To the conclusions drawn by Rick Warren and the others of like minds, there will be no denial or debate from me. In fact wholeheartedly, I concur with Rick Warren and the others that Biblically, they are absolutely accurate. Indeed, God does have purpose for man's existence which includes bountiful blessings.

The Creation story clearly indicates these facts. First, God created man to relate to him. Genesis says, "God came down in the cool of the day to converse with Adam and Eve" (Genesis 3: 8 KJV). God created mankind for fellowship. The second observation of the Creation story is that God created man to represent (or re-present) God in the earth. The third observation is that God created man to bless him.

The second and third observations are easily confirmed in Genesis 1: 28. Moses wrote, "God blessed them and said to them, "Be fruitful and increase in number; fill the earth and subdue it. Rule over the fish of the sea and the birds of the air and over every living creature that moves on the ground.

Then God said, "I give you every seed-bearing plant on the face of the whole earth and every tree that has fruit with seed in it. They will be yours for food. And to all the beasts of the earth and all the birds of the air and all the creatures that move on the ground, everything that has the breath of life in it, I give every green plant for food: And it was so" (Gen. 1: 28-30 NIV).

So there it is, written, God blessed mankind with every necessary gift for happiness and fulfillment. Yet, bursting at the seams to be heard is the most agonizing question of history. It wants to know what happened: What took man from the state of blissful jubilation to his current reality of misery, pain and strife? What interrupted his peace, tranquility and love of, and for life?

The answer was located just two chapters from the Creation story. In the book of Genesis, chapter three, for the first time in history, mankind met his arch-enemy: The enemy of God and man that not only wants mankind beaten and broken, but destroyed.

The hearing of these words, even some six thousands biblical years later still sends chills down the spine. One can only imagine the emotions of Adam and Eve at the discovery; the shock must have been "off of the charts."

Think about it, seemingly out of the blue, the discovery is made of an enemy of such proportional hatred and destruction: One that you have not known and certainly have not caused any hurt or harm. Yet, the enemy not only wants you hurt, but dead, both physically and spiritually.

Not only would this information shock you; it would be horrifying. Genesis 3: 1 introduced such a personality as the Serpent, but is better known today as the Devil or Satan. There will be more specific details on the Devil in chapter III, entitled, who is the Devil?

For the record, I am well aware of the fact that there are many books written about the existence of the Devil. To be exact, there are so many books written on the subject that it would take this entire book to name them all.

However, the purpose of this book is not simply to offer proof of the existence of the Devil, nor just to characterize his behavior: It was written to offer a deep and detailed study on his existence, as well as on his origin, objectives and role in the affairs of human beings. Further, it was written to lay out the evidence of his involvement and offer Biblical strategies to defeat his efforts to destroy the human family.

Surprisingly, there are millions of people walking the face of the earth that do not believe in the existence of the Devil. According to a Gallup Poll article, entitled, More Americans Believe in God and Heaven than in the Devil and Hell; taken May 10-13, 2007, indicating that only 78% of Americans believe in God.

However, when measuring Americans' belief in the Devil, Gallup poll results revealed that more Americans believe in the Devil this year compared to 1990 when only 55 percent believed in the existence of the Devil. Still the number of Americans that do not believe in the existence of the Devil is staggering.

Yet the most staggering aspect of the numbers occurs when faces are plugged into the numbers. By themselves, the cold and hard numbers of statistics don't mean much and certainly don't do much to move men and women; but add the names and faces and immediately mankind's emotions change.

As a pastor for more than thirty years, I know this to be factual. Everyday of every week, I call the names and meet the faces behind the numbers. I see first hand, the impact and the result of man's disbelief in the existence of the Devil.

One of the major results of the disbelief is directly related to the low numbers of those that attend church regularly. According to the U. S. Census Bureau of 2006 taken for Greenville County of South Carolina; the population was 417, 166.

Of this number, 80% did not attend church on a regular basis. The actual number of people not attending church was 333, 732. The number is astounding any where in the nation, but particularly so, in the region called the "Bible Belt."

The national percentages are similar. According to the *American Sociological Review*, v. 63 (1998): 137-145 (with L. Stinson). Comparing diaries with actual attendance, they made the estimate that the actual percentage of Americans attending church from the mid-1960's to the 90's was about 26%.

The number of Americans that believe in God and don't believe in the Devil is absolutely astonishing. (I suspect the numbers are similar with people all around the globe). The astonishment is accompanied by the fact that the same God within the same Bible, the same chapter and the same verse declares the existence of both God and the Devil.

For instance, the book of Job says, "One day the angels came to present themselves before the LORD, and Satan also came with them. The LORD said to Satan, "Where have you come from?" Satan answered the LORD, "From roaming through the earth and going back and forth in it" (Job 1: 6-7, NIV).

The same can be said of the controversy concerning heaven and hell. Jesus speaks of them both in the sixteenth chapter of Luke, beginning at verse 19. Although he speaks of heaven as being in the bosom of Abraham, yet it is clear that he is speaking of the heavenly bliss of man's final state. He says to the rich man who "in hell, lifted up his eyes, being in torments" that there is a great gulf fixed that divides the two separate final resting places (Luke 16: 19-31 KJV).

Also the existence of both heaven and hell is stated in the gospel of Matthew. Jesus says in verse 9, "And if your eye causes you to sin, gouge it out and throw it away. It is better for you to enter life with one eye than to have two eyes and be thrown into the fire of hell. See that you do not look down on one of these little ones. For I tell you that their angels in heaven always see the face of my Father in heaven" Matt. 18: 9-10 NIV).

The book of the Revelation of Jesus, which he gave unto his servant, John, declares the existence of both heaven and hell in chapters 20-21. Yet there are many people that believe in heaven and don't believe in hell. It is simply astonishing, even illogical and irrational since the Bible repeatedly declares them both.

The incredible irrationality of this position must be addressed. People need to start reading their Bibles and stop basing their beliefs are feelings. Man needs to be reminded that the initial concept of heaven came to the men and women of this generation through the pages of the Bible. If it had not been for Jesus Christ who gave man the revelation and the writers of the Bible that passed it on to us, we would not have the knowledge of heaven.

Man's knowledge of hell came through the same process, so to deny the existence of one and not the other is inconsistent with logical thinking. It is irrational. According to Webster's dictionary, the word irrational means, incapable of reason. In other words, man can not have one without the other. No Hell; No Heaven: No Heaven; No Hell.

Clearly, reality reveals mankind's lack of knowledge about the Devil, which highlights the world's critical need for education in this area. God said to Hosea, "My people are destroyed for a lack of knowledge" (Hosea 4: 6 KJV). Jesus said, "And ye shall know the truth, and the truth shall make you free" (John 8: 32 KJV).

It's like being lost in the mountains and there is only one way out to freedom. You have to be on the right road, heading in the right direction to reach it. All of the other roads lead to dead ends. Truth then is the reality of being on the one right path, heading in the right direction and that will make you free.

The necessity of writing this book is to inform mankind of the one right path to defeat the Devil. In short summary, herein lie the premise of the book; **If mankind is enlightened enough to acknowledge the Devil's existence, recognize his actions of evil toward them as individuals and mankind in general, defeat him in their daily walk of experience by relying on God's Word and the Holy Spirit, as did Jesus, they can and will live abundant, peaceful and fulfilling lives.**

Example: Out in the wilderness of Jordan, after Jesus acknowledged, recognized and defeated the Devil, he was fulfilled and energized. The Bible says, "When the devil had finished all this tempting, he left him until an opportune time. Jesus returned to Galilee in the "power of the

Spirit," and news about him spread through the whole countryside. He taught in their synagogues, and everyone praised him" (Luke 4: 13-15, NIV).

In the Upper room, Jesus said to Peter, "Simon, Simon, Satan desires to have you that he may sift you as wheat, but I am praying for you that your faith fail not: and when you are returned to me, strengthen your brothers (Luke 22: 31, NKJV).

God's plans for mankind are clear in the Word that he wants us to live blessed and abundant lives. It is also clear in the Word that the Devil does not. Jesus could not have made this point clearer than he did in the gospel of John. He said, "The Thief comest not, but for to steal, and to kill and to destroy: I am come that they might have life, and that they might have it more abundantly" (John 10: 10, KJV).

Therefore, the ability to acknowledge the Devil's existence, recognize him in the everyday experiences of life and resist his temptations are the keys to success and literally, can change one's life.

On the other hand, the inability to acknowledge, recognize and defeat the Devil will destroy lives. Mankind will continue wrestling against flesh and blood, fighting against and even killing one another and devastation will continue, "Business as usual." Somebody said, "If you think education cost, try ignorance."

Think about the price that mankind has paid because of his ignorance of the Devil. Had Eve (who sinned first) and Adam acknowledged the Devil, recognized his disguise as the serpent (Gen. 3: 1) and resisted his temptation, their lives and ours would be very different today.

There would be no death, pain or sorrow and the world would not be as treacherous as we know it. At least in Adam and Eve's favor, they could argue, truthfully that they had not heard of the enemy before they were deceived, an argument that you and I can not make today.

Moreover, had Judas Iscariot acknowledged and recognized Satan and resisted him (Luke 22: 3); he would not have committed suicide when his plan of Jesus' betrayal failed. At Caesarea Philippi, had Peter acknowledged and recognized Satan (as did Jesus, Matthew 16: 23) and resisted him, he would not have allowed Satan to lead him to deny Jesus, not once or twice, but three times.

Larry Huch, in his book, entitled, "10 Curses that Block the Blessings," makes an interesting analogy of Peter's denial and restoration. In the denial, Peter; first, denied Jesus to a young girl (Matt. 26: 69). In the restoration of Peter, Jesus first question to him was as follows: the Scripture says, "When they had finished eating, Jesus said to Simon Peter, "Simon son of John, do you truly love me more than these?" "Yes, Lord," he said, "you know that I love you." Jesus said, "Feed my lambs" or remember the children (John 21: 15 NIV).

In the denial, the second and third groups of people to question Peter were adults. In the restoration, Jesus said to Peter a second and third time, "Simon son of John, do you truly love me?" He answered, "Yes, Lord, you know that I love you." Jesus said, "Take care of my sheep" (John 21: 16 NIV) referring to the adults.

This is a reminder that God is taking note of every activity of man; even the simplicity of a conversation with a young child is not overlooked. Jesus said, "But I say unto you, That every idle word that men shall speak, they shall give account thereof in the day of judgment. For by thy words thou shalt be justified, and by thy words thou shalt be condemned" (Matt. 12: 36-37 KJV).

Paul said, "Whatsoever a man soweth, that shall he also reap" (Gal. 6: 7 KJV). For "what goes up; must come down," "what goes around; comes around." What is planted today; will sprout tomorrow. Therefore, sow good seeds and reap good harvests.

Oh, what differences it would make in men and women's lives today, if they would acknowledge, recognize and resist the Devil's influence.

There is absolutely no excuse for mankind not to do so. The ability to resist him is within us. James said so. He said, "Resist the Devil and he will flee from you" (James 4: 7 KJV).

Speaking of the Devil, Peter said, "Resist him, standing firm in the faith, because you know that your brothers throughout the world are undergoing the same kind of sufferings. And the God of all grace, who called you to his eternal glory in Christ, after you have suffered a little while, will himself restore you and make you strong, firm and steadfast" (I Peter 5: 9-10 NIV).

Paul said the same: "Put on the full armor of God so that you can take your stand against the devil's schemes (Ephesians 6: 11 NIV). If the ability to resist the Devil was not within mankind, Jesus would not have commanded them to do so.

Once again, it is critically imperative that an examination be done and adhered on the Devil and the destructive role that he plays in human history. It is simply incredible how he has managed for so long to go obscured, unnoticed and without scrutiny. With all of the evil and devastation that has come and gone and currently face the world, it's amazing that there are not more people and entities engaged in research on the cause.

However, I believe that if the subject is seriously studied, the conclusion will be obvious: the Devil is most responsible for the evil experienced by the human family. So much so that before God and Christ set up the new heaven and the new earth, they will rid themselves of the Devil by destroying him in the Lake of Fire (Rev. 20: 10 KJV). To me that act of the Godhead speaks volumes.

Stay tuned to the station of the book, 1;1;1. The old preacher said, one for the Father, one for the Son and one for the Holy Spirit. The next chapter will take us on another safari, further into the dark jungles of the Devil's domain in search of the unknown. It will assess evil and tragedy in the world and its source.

But before moving on to the next chapter, write down at least three tidbits of information learned from the above chapter.

1._____

2._____

3._____

CHAPTER II

THE DEVIL AND EVIL: TWO PEAS IN A POD!

AN ASSESSMENT OF EVIL AND ITS SOURCE!

"You are from your father the devil, and you choose to do your father's desires. He was a murderer from the beginning and does not stand in the truth, because there is no truth in him. When he lies, he speaks according to his own nature, for he is a liar and the father of lies" (John 8: 44 NRSV).

Think about some of the world tragedies of late history. Who can forget these major headliners? In April 20, 1999, the massacre at Columbine high school where 12 students, a teacher and 23 others were shot. It ended with the two shooters committing suicide. [1]

The Virginia Tech. Massacre occurred April 16, 2007: 32 innocent people were gun-downed by a student named Cho. [2] A trench coat clad teenager killed five people and wounded four others, before being fatally shot by police at a mall in Utah. He calmly aimed shotgun at helpless victims, witnesses' said.[3]

June 21-2003, From the Bangkok Post: "On June 6, Nung, a high school boy in Pakpanang School in Nakhon Si Thammarat fired at school mates after morning assembly. Two were killed and many others were injured. The boy testified that he was aiming at a classmate with whom he had a raw (argument)." [4]

Two days later, June 8, Bangkok student Panumas Sutthinan went on a rampage at his ex-girl friend's house killing her uncle and grandmother before turning the gun on himself. He was reportedly angry over the ending of the relationship." [5]

The list of massacres and tragedies that have shocked our world, even in recent history is massive and extensive. In comparison, the list of personal and local tragedies is just as traumatizing. From a pastoral point of view, everyday, someone I know experiences a personal family crisis.

Just recently, a mother was forced to bury her son, who was shot and killed by his girl friend for a reason as frivolous as finding an unknown telephone number in his wallet.

Other tragedies include a man that shot and killed an acquaintance over a few dollars in a gambling dispute. A mother left two small children at home alone for days while partying wildly with friends. Tragically, the house caught on fire leaving both of the children dead. Unfortunately, there is not enough time and space to mention the untold number of adults that have left children in hot automobiles for hours with tragic results.

The skyrocketing divorce rate is another subject with its own set of problems, causing division in the home between children and parents. The U. S. Census Bureau and the National Care for Health Statistics reported that in the year 2000, 41% of the couples married, ended in divorce.

The percentage is scary by itself, but when the actual number of yearly divorces is plugged into the total (**957, 200**) it becomes a nightmare for the stability of society.

The research done on the tragedy of divorce indicates a serious moral decline. According to a 2001 Barna Research Poll, 33 percent of born-again Christians ended their marriages in divorce, roughly the same as the general population, and 90 percent of those divorces happen AFTER the conversion to Christianity.

This is sad news for the Church (Body of Baptized believers in Christ). It indicates that the church is not a sanctuary from evil and social unrest. Neither is it exempt from the temptations and tests of the Devil.

Further proof of the church's ineffectiveness is demonstrated by the fact that not only is the divorce rate out of control both in society and in the Church, the rate of Church fights and split ups are out of control as well.

In an Internet's coverage of an AME church fight in St. Paul Minnesota; this fact was demonstrated. While being interviewed on a national broadcast network by Mr. Walter Furly, the video showed a female church trustee physically attacking the pastor. It showed her slapping him and him returning the favor and pandemonium breaking out.

Unfortunately, the fight in the AME church was not an isolated event, acts of this nature are occurring all over the nation and in every denomination.

In the past 30 years, I have pastored five churches in the Baptist denomination and witnessed, first hand, the Devil's destructive influence.

So much so that the evil experienced at my last pastorate by the Devil caused me to re-evaluate my ideology and theology concerning the traditional family dominated church.

It left me with many questions and doubts, such as; can there be an effective ministry and uncompromised biblical proclamation of Jesus to a lost world in the traditional family dominated church? By this, I mean the church where a few families dominate the leadership and the direction of the church.

I realize that the majority of churches, if not all of them have a few dominant families that founded or better yet, organized the church. I also realize that most all of these churches were organized by the founding father's sincerity and righteousness.

However, over the course of time, the process of passing the leadership torch of righteousness was flawed. The new leaders were not chosen because of their spirituality (as directed by Scripture in Acts 6: 3, etc,). Thus, the church has been left in dire need of spiritual guidance and direction.

Even with this consideration, the situation would still not be so problematic, if the majority of the church members would recognize this flaw and take the necessary action to restore the church's spirituality. In many of the church's leadership positions, the lack of spirituality is not hidden, but out in the open and clearly seen.

Let it be clearly understood that I am not suggesting that all of the church officers are not spiritual. To the contrary, in some of the churches, there are some strong officers in the Lord that understand their roles.

Unfortunately, there are others that do not and it's clear that they are not following the direction of the Holy Spirit. The church must very seriously consider the immeasurable damage that's being inflicted on the church and the work of God by these non-spirit filled persons.

Someone reading this book may wonder; how I can make such an assessment of people's spiritual condition? I can do so and so can you by the authority of the written Word of God. The written Word informs us of the character of people led by the Spirit versus those led by the flesh.

Paul said, "So I say, live by the Spirit, and you will not gratify the desires of the sinful nature. For the sinful nature desires what is contrary to the Spirit; and the Spirit what is contrary to the sinful nature. They are in conflict with each other, so that you do not do what you want.

But if you are led by the Spirit, you are not under law. The acts of the sinful nature are obvious: sexual immorality, impurity and debauchery; idolatry and witchcraft; hatred, discord, jealousy, fits of rage, selfish ambition, dissensions, factions and envy; drunkenness, orgies, and the like. I warn you, as I did before, that those who live like this will not inherit the kingdom of God.

But the fruit of the Spirit is love, joy, peace, patience, kindness, goodness, faithfulness, gentleness and self-control. Against such things there is no law" (Galatians 5: 16-23, NIV). Jesus said, "Make a tree good and its fruit will be good, or make a tree bad and its fruit will be bad, for a tree is recognized by its fruit" (Matthew 12: 33 NIV).

Therefore the question, whether or not there can be effective ministry and uncompromised biblical proclamation of Jesus to a lost world in the churches of this sort is un-clear to many. For there are those that declare in the affirmative and say yes, there can.

To them, the question becomes one of percentage: what percentage of effective ministry and proper proclamation can be done. Are five, ten, twenty, or even fifty percent of effective ministry and proper proclamation satisfactory? Can the world be affected spiritually with only a fifty percent performance of affective ministry by the Church?

There needs to be given more consideration to the many meetings with officers and church leaders that far too often diminish spiritual goals and accomplishments. Though let it be said loudly that there is nothing wrong with the process of meeting, but there is something seriously wrong with the people conducting the process without spiritual goals.

The church leadership must always remember that Jesus said, "He who is not with me is against me; and he who does not gather with me scatters abroad" (Matt. 12: 30 NKJV T.D. Jakes). Church leaders must also remember that either, "they are part of the solution or part of the problem."

There is no middle ground on which to stand or fence to straddle. Jesus said to the church at Laodicea, "So, because you are lukewarm--neither hot nor cold--I am about to spit you out of my mouth" (Rev. 3: 16 NIV).

Therefore the question is raised again, can there be effective ministry and uncompromised Biblical proclamation of Jesus to a lost world in the churches of this nature? Though un-clear to many, the answer is clear to some. It's clear enough for this pastor and the many other pastors of like minds and experiences to organize churches without these confining and restrictive barriers.

Churches free of the long standing traditions of men (one of the areas most comforting to the Devil). It was the need for education in this area that provided much of the motivation to write this book.

Remember, the caution of Jesus to the church at Sardis, "Thou hast a name that thou livest, and art dead" (Rev. 3: 1b KJV). To the church at Pergamos, it was, "I know thy works and where thou dwellest, even where Satan's seat is" (Rev. 2: 13a KJV).

Once again, remember Jesus' words: "To the angel of the church in Laodicea write: These are the words of the Amen, the faithful and true witness, the ruler of God's creation. I know your deeds, that you are neither cold nor hot. I wish you were either one or the other! So, because you are lukewarm--neither hot nor cold--I am about to spit you out of my mouth" (Rev. 3: 14-16 NIV).

In fact, the book of Revelation records seven letters that Jesus wrote to seven churches. Five of those letters written to the churches contained serious indictments against the church: The need to write the letters in the first place indicated the seriousness of the church's assessment by Jesus. Lest man forgets, Jesus' greatest opposition came from the traditions of religious men. In modern terminology, Jesus' greatest opposition came from "Church folk."

Matthew 15 records one of the many such conflicts. "The Scribes and Pharisees came to Jesus asking him about the disciples not washing their hands before eating bread according to the traditions of the elders. Jesus asked them, why do ye also transgress the commandment of God by your traditions?

Jesus continued the discussion with them about the command of God concerning honor of their fathers and mothers. Verse six basically summed up his scolding of them. He said, "Thus you have made the commandment of God of none effect by your tradition? Ye hypocrite, Isaiah prophesied of you" (Matthew 15: 1-7).

This confrontation and many others of similarity demonstrate Jesus' disdain for the traditions of religious men. So men and women of religion and tradition; be cautious about your legislation.

It goes without saying that there are many burdens resting squarely on the shoulders of the church. The greatest (and one that is least emphasized) is its duty to consistently remind itself of its responsibility for existence.

The greatest reason for the existence of the church is to promote Christ and righteousness in a non-Christian and un-righteous world. It sounds simple, yet, in many churches, the reason for existence has been corrupted.

So, let all of the church leaders around the world be reminded that Jesus founded the church and it still belongs to Him. He said, "And I tell you that you are Peter, and on this rock I will build my church, and the gates of Hades will not overcome it" (Matt. 16: 18 NIV). Earlier, he had said, "Seek ye first the kingdom of God and his righteousness; and all these things shall be added unto you" (Matt. 6: 33 KJV).

Therefore, in its effort to promote Christ, the church has no option, but to deal with the Devil and the demons of damnation. (There will be more on the Devil's influence on man in chapter IV, entitled, "Who Really is the Devil?") Without knowledge of the Devil, there can not be effective ministries or the proper proclamation of Jesus to a lost world. God said, "My people are destroyed for a lack of knowledge" (Hosea 4: 6 KJV).

Because of this lack of knowledge and understanding, everywhere one look in the world today, evil is occurring with great regularity. So much so, that a prompting of new psychological studies on the subject of evil has been initiated.

Even the mass news media's reports reflect the newfound attitude and concerns. Everyday, an explanation is asserted by somebody as to the hidden reasons behind the many tragedies and massacres.

In America, the most reported conclusion suggests the lack of gun control laws and the unlimited amount of violence and corruption seen on television as the cause. Psychologically, that conclusion is feasible, however theologically, "the math just doesn't add up."

While, it may be true that the lack of gun control laws and the unlimited amount of violence and corruption seen on television may play some part in the instigation of these tragedies and may even be symptomatic of a psychologically sick society, however, neither of these positions should shoulder the burden for the presence of evil in America.

In fact, the small list of the tragedies provided previously, indicate a couple of things. First, the problems of evil are not isolated to American soil. The problems of evil are worldwide and occurring in nations around the globe.

Second, the solution is not solved by stricter laws of gun control and regulation of television violence and corruption. The evidence of this is as clear as crystal; other nations have more strict laws of gun control and more regulation of television violence and corruption than America, yet evil, violence and corruption still resides on the sands of their shores.

Unquestionably, the evidence shows that these are not the source of tragedy, violence and evil. So, the question of the source of evil and tragedy remain. If the source is neither of the above, what is? Or maybe the framing of the question should be changed. Maybe the question should not be what, but *WHO* is the source? Could it be the *WILL*, *WORK* and *INFLUENCE* of the Devil?

Be reminded of the Purpose and Premise of this book.

First, the Purpose: The book was not written simply to offer proof of the existence of the Devil, or to just characterize his behavior. It was written to offer a deep and detailed study on his existence, yes, but also on his origin, objectives and role in the affairs of human beings. Further, it was written to lay out the evidence of his involvement and offer biblical strategies to defeat his efforts to destroy the human family.

Second, the Premise: _if mankind is enlightened enough to acknowledge the Devil's existence, recognize his actions of evil toward them as individuals and mankind in general, defeat him in their daily walk of experience by relying on God's Word and the Holy Spirit, as did Jesus, they can and will live abundant, peaceful and fulfilling lives.

Make note that since the Devil's introduction to mankind (Genesis 3: 1) more than 6000 years of Biblical history has passed, yet he is just as dangerous and deadly today as ever. The reason for this must be addressed. Galatians 6: 7a, God warned man to "be not deceived, God is not mocked."

For it was the deliberate action of the Serpent (Devil) that led Eve (who sinned first) and Adam into sin and death. The names of the players may have changed, but the goal of the Devil's game remains the same.

Just for the record, please note what the topic of discussion is here. It is about the source of tragedy and evil. It is not about their creation. There are major differences between the two subjects and the latter will be discussed in more detail in chapter V, Who is God?

However, please note that Webster defines source as the cause of a thing being present [6] and not necessarily why the thing exists. For example, when asking the question about the source of the water on the kitchen floor, obviously, the question is not about the creation of the water on the floor.

Likewise is the discourse taking place here: The focal point of the discussion is not about the creation of evil. Although, if a poll was taken, based upon my 30 year pastoral experience, it would reveal that many people think that the Devil created evil. As many think, the Devil created death, Hell and the grave (which also will be discussed later in chapter V).

The exegesis of the Biblical text proves beyond the shadow of a doubt that the Devil did not create evil. (The word exegesis is one that is used frequently; thereby a short definition of it might be helpful to the reader. It is a detailed study and research of a text, to fully understand its meaning.)

Thus the doctrine that the Devil created evil must be denied with adamancy. **The Devil did not create evil! The Devil did not create evil! The Devil did not create evil!** Have I said it enough? One more time, **The Devil did not create evil!** In fact, please note that the Devil is not a creator. The Devil himself is a created being.

Admittedly the Devil was not created the Devil or Satan (the adversary of God in Greek language and thought); nonetheless, the Devil was still created. He was created an archangel and Lucifer was his name. There will be more on the origin of the Devil in chapter IV.

Categorically, it is being stated here that there is but one Creator and Jehovah God is His known name. The Scripture clearly indicates that He is the only Creator (Genesis 1: 1; Colossians 1: 16; Isaiah 40: 28).

As such, there is but one conclusion to be drawn and drank from the well of truth, **God created evil.** Isaiah 45 records the following words: "I form the light and create darkness: I make peace and create evil: I the Lord do all these things" (Isaiah 45: 7 KJV).

The Proverbs of Solomon records, "The Lord hath made all things for himself: yea, even the wicked for the day of evil" (Proverbs 16: 4 KJV & RV). As debated and unpopular as that maybe for some people to accept, nonetheless; it is the truth, the whole truth and nothing but the truth, so help me God.

Just think about this for a moment: If God for his own reasons created death, hell, and the grave, why is it so difficult to believe that he created evil. (There will be more discussion on this subject in chapter V, who is God?)

In fact, the writing of this book came from the inspiration of God. The goal of it is to **re-focus man's attention to the Devil, God, and man himself.** It was written to give men and women an understanding of why they really do what they do.

One of the prepositions of the book is that men and women do not know why they do what they do. It is acknowledged that they think that they do, but when placed under the microscopic lens of examination, it is revealed that the majority of people really do not. (This subject will be addressed later in chapter seven, entitled, "Why I really do what I do?)

First, the attention of the book is centered on shining the spotlight on the Devil, highlighting his agenda and bringing his conniving ways out of the closet into the public eye.

Far too long, he has been instigating havoc, throwing rocks of destruction and hiding his hand. Inside of the courtrooms of law, a witness takes the oath and testifies that he/she will tell "the truth, the whole truth and nothing but the truth, so help me God." I take the same oath, "to tell the truth, the whole truth and nothing but the truth on the Devil, so help me God."

Having declared that and so committed; let us continue. Every time I am privy to a discussion about the condition of the world and all of the possible reasons for the evil, I am overwhelmed and amazed that the Devil's name is rarely mentioned in the conversation.

On the few occasions that it is mentioned, it is mentioned with disdain for the people that would suggest such an improbable possibility. What makes this negative attitude and the omission of the Devil's participation more amazing and mind-boggling is mankind's known love affair with investigation.

The choice not to investigate the Devil and his possible involvement in the evil of the world is not only mind-boggling; but reckless and inexplicable. Especially when taken into consideration the love that human beings hold for investigations, studies, examinations, polls and surveys.

In any discussion, whenever there is a question about any subject and no answer is presented, inevitably, a human will make a motion that a study needs to be done.

Everyday, studies, polls, surveys, research and investigations are done on practically every subject under the sun. So much so today, that almost all entities have their own department for studies, poll taking, investigation and research. Even the ant has its share of study, investigation and research: "The Study of Ants." [7] Just to name one.

If monies are spent on the research of the ant, why not spend some money researching the Devil and his involvement in tragedy? Every time a person expires, there is money spent on an autopsy. There are huge amounts of money spent on the research of AIDS, Cancer, Diabetes, etc; as there should. But also, money needs to be spent on the research of the Devil's involvement in tragedy and destruction.

As the premise of the book repeatedly indicates, there should be research done on how to **enlighten mankind enough to acknowledge the Devil's existence, recognize his actions of evil toward them as individuals and mankind in general, defeat him in the daily walk of experience by relying on God's Word and the Holy Spirit, as did Jesus, in order that Human Beings can and will live abundant, peaceful and fulfilling lives.**

The omission of the Devil from investigation and in particular, his role and involvement in the devastation of the world is outrageously irrational. It makes no sense. It is a deliberate act of genocide given the knowledge that's available to man about the Devil. The majority of men already know, but for those that do not know, Satan is a murderer, Jesus said so in John 8: 44.

Also, the world knows that he is a thief that comes only to steal, kill and destroy (John 10: 10). More attention will be given to this in the chapter, entitled, "Who is the Devil?" Still, the decision not to investigate the Devil is highly suspicious.

But, before the chapter ends, briefly, there's another mandatory point to be made on the Devil's craftiness and cunning in the world. It will be discussed later in greater detail, but a word is needed here. *The world's failure to include the Devil in the investigative process and exempt him from the interrogation lineup could NOT be accidental.*

It is deliberate and strategic: There is a massive cover-up taking place and the Devil is the mastermind behind it. Given the Devil's forte in history, the conclusion that I have presented should not be surprising. The Devil has a long history of "Throwing rocks and hiding his hand: digging ditches and setting traps."

A case in point is recorded in the Gospel of Luke. Satan did all of the above to Jesus in Luke 22. The Bible says, "**Then entered Satan into Judas, surnamed, Iscariot,** being a number of the twelve. And he went his way and communed with the chief Priests and captains, how he might betray him (Jesus) unto them" (Luke 22: 3-4 KJV).

Clearly Satan was involved in the plot to arrest, try and crucify Jesus: As he was in the attacked of Job (Job 1-2) and Adam and Eve (Genesis 3: 1). Whether or not it is known by the masses, my task is to make the Devil's involvement common knowledge: For he has gone too long obscured and without scrutiny.

Like his anonymity in the plot to crucify Jesus, for more than six thousand years, the Devil has been actively wreaking havoc in the lives of men and women. Unfortunately to mankind's own detriment, man doesn't seem to have been listening or paying much attention to the cause behind the scene of the tragedies.

The question is, reader, are you listening to God's voice and paying attention to the evil that the Devil is stirring up in your life? The Devil is in the world, everyday, causing you problems and seeking havoc and destruction. His desires, suggestions and influence are all geared toward hurting the human race.

By picking up this book and reading it, you have made a great effort toward understanding the mindset of the Devil. Hopefully, you will gain knowledge and increase your vision to the point of automatic recognition of the Devil and the demonic activity surrounding you and change your life.

Again, be reminded of the Purpose and Premise of the book. They are as follows: First the Purpose, the book was not written simply to offer proof of the existence of the Devil, or to just characterize his behavior. It was written to offer a deep and detailed study on his existence, yes, but also on his origin, objectives and role in the affairs of Human Beings. Further, it was written to lay out the evidence of his involvement and offer biblical strategies to defeat his efforts to destroy the human family.

Second, the premise: If mankind is enlightened enough to acknowledge the Devil's existence, recognize his actions of evil toward them as individuals and mankind in general, defeat him in their daily walk of experience by relying on God's Word, as did Jesus, they can and will live abundant, peaceful and fulfilling lives.

My prayer to God and hope for the nation is that, in the twenty first Century, mankind will wakeup and smell the coffee. So world, wake up, read up and gird up. In order that we may see things as they are really are. Chapter Two: A word about the theme: Did the Devil make me do it?

But before moving on to the next chapter, write down at least three tidbits of information learned from the above chapter.

1._____

2._____

3._____

CHAPTER III

A WORD ABOUT THE THEME!

A TRIP DOWN MEMORY LANE

"The man said, "The woman whom you gave to be with me, she gave me fruit from the tree, and I ate." Then the LORD God said to the woman, "What is this that you have done?" The woman said, "The serpent tricked me, and I ate" (Gen. 3: 11-12 NRSV).

In September of 1970, a comedian named Flip Wilson launched the Flip Wilson show. The show is well remembered for several reasons. First, it is well remembered because it was one of the first successful net-work variety series starring an African American: At the time, this was a significant fact. It concretely etched into the stonework of history that African Americans could not only become successful television personalities, but have the starring roles.

For hundreds of years, previously, the Devil used divisions of race, creed, color, sex, denomination and every thing else to deceive man into disunity. Racism, classism, sexism and denominationalism are but a few of the methods that the Devil used to divide man, hoping for his destruction.

Today, let man be aware that the Devil still uses whatever he can to divide mankind. The Devil knows that a divided house, people, church and anything else cannot stand.

The supportive evidence of this presupposition comes directly from the Word of God. "But Jesus knew their thoughts and said to them: "Every kingdom divided against it-self is brought to desolation and every city or house divided against itself will not stand. If Satan cast out Satan, he is divided against himself, how then will his kingdom stand?" (Matt. 12: 25-26, NKJV).

However, it's intriguing to examine, racism and how it became the most divisive tactic used by the Devil for the last four hundred years. It's even more intriguing to discover that the word race can not be found written on the Biblical pages of history. This discovery resonates in high definition that God has not endorsed racism nor uttered the word *race* (in terms of people).

If racism did not come from God, where did it come from? This is a great question worthy of examination and will be answered shortly. But one thing is crystal clear, God does not endorse it. The subjects of concern that God Biblically endorses are words like family, belonging, unity and the commonality of the human creation.

Through the mouth of the prophets and the preachers, the following words remind us of God's position. Paul said, "God hath made of **one blood** all nations of men for to dwell on all the face of the earth" (Acts 17: 26; KJV).

Peter said, "Of a truth, I perceive that God is no respecter of persons: but **in every nation,** he that feareth him and worketh righteousness is accepted with him" (Acts 10: 34 KJV).

Paul said to the Romans, "For there is **no difference between the Jew and the Greek**: for the same Lord over all is rich unto all that call upon him. For whosoever shall call upon the name of the Lord shall be saved" (Romans 10: 12-13 KJV).

Paul said to the Galatians, "There is neither **Jew nor Greek, there is neither bond nor free, there is neither male nor female:** for ye are all one in Christ Jesus" (Gal. 3: 28 KJV). Clearly, racism was not of God. Pope Benedict XVI said this: "namely, that there is only *one* humanity in the many human beings. The Bible says a decisive "No" to all racism and to every human division."[8] So the puzzling question remains, if God didn't do it, who did?

The only way to put a puzzle together, you've got to have all of the pieces. The only possible answer to the puzzle of racism is that it is a concoction of the Devil: Used with one goal in mind to destroy the human family by further dividing man physically and intellectually.

It seemed like before the 1970's, the above passages were either not well known or simply, just weren't followed. On the verdict of the African American's mental capacity for intellectual achievement, the jury was still out.

Surprisingly some on the jury, wrestling with the question were African American themselves. The culprit of low self-esteem passed down from generation to generation has hindered African American's progress since the days of slavery.

But thank God, the question of the African American's intelligence was not considered by all. Great milestones were achieved in the sixties that strengthened African Americans beliefs in themselves. Surely, the Devil's use of racism was dying a slow death.

Today, more and more people are coming to new understandings and alliances with the truth. The truth as collaborated in the Declaration of Independence by the founding fathers of this nation: "We hold these truths to be self-evident that all men are created equal, that they are endowed by their Creator with certain unalienable Rights that among these are life, liberty and the pursuit of happiness."

Then, surprisingly in April, 2008, racism regained its nerve and raised its ugly hand for recognition. It stood up on the floor of America and offered a motion that Blacks support Blacks and Whites support Whites. Racism became such an issue that Senator Barak Obama (a Black democratic presidential candidate), addressed the nation on the subject and its continued divisiveness.

However, the majority of Americans need to be commended for their vote to defeat the motion of racism. By doing so, their act became a historic moment in the political movement of humanity toward equality and the eradication of the most divisive weapon in the Devil's arsenal for fueling division in America.

So much so that in June of 2008, Senator Barak Obama became the presumptive democratic nominee for the presidency of the United States of America. He became the first African American to reach such a height in American History. America; truly lived up its name, The United States of America.

While, many in the Democratic Primary (White, Black, Hispanic and others) overcame the race issue, sadly there were others that did not. Once again, there were too many (White, Black, Hispanic and others) that fell victim to the device of the Devil, racism.

Apparently, on the issue of racism, human beings are slow learners. In fact, human beings are slow learners altogether of the devices of the Devil. Paul warned us, "Lest Satan should get an advantage of us: for we are not ignorant of his devices" (II Cor. 2: 11 KJV). In order not to be ignorant of the devices of the Devil, the need for education concerning him is great.

Which leads me to the second reason for the fond memories of the Flip Wilson Show; it popularized the phrase, **"The Devil made me do it."**

For those too young to remember, the phrase was birthed during the seventies on this show.

If memory serves me well, there was a single, sassy and somewhat modernized woman named Geraldine Jones (portrayed by Flip Wilson) that uttered the phrase each time after being caught in a compromising position.

The plot of the show thickened when it was revealed that Geraldine Jones dated a man named Killer. The name Killer, in and of it-self should have raised eyebrows of concern for her well-being. Additionally to that, the fact that he was consistently in and out of prison made matters worst.

These facts alone should have tried, convicted and sentenced the relationship to the death penalty: A wise person would not be involved in such a relationship. The Bible teaches, "And he said to humankind, 'Truly, the fear of the Lord, that is wisdom; and to depart from evil is understanding'" (Job 28: 28 NRSV).

Unfortunately however, Geraldine Jones did not exercise good understanding, the relationship not only survived, it thrived. For some reason, there are people that like (no, love) living dangerously.

But the old folk used to say, "If you play with fire, you are bound to get burned. If you sling mud, you are going to get some on you. Don't throw rocks, if you live in a glass house." The message is, choose your friends carefully, particularly your boy/girl friend and husband/ wife.

From June of 2001 until March of 2006, I served on the South Carolina Board of Juvenile Probation and Parole. It was there that I became aware of a new law that the young people in particular need to be aware of. It states,

"The hand of one is the hand of them all." This means that if you are with somebody that violates the law and you don't prevent them, you will be considered a participant in the criminal behavior, even though;

personally you did not commit the crime. Again, choose your friends and riding buddies very carefully. The legal thought is, "birds of feather flock together."

The name Killer (and all of what that implies), in addition to the fact that when not in jail or confinement, he was a permanent presence at the pool hall; still did not end the romance with Ms. Jones. The Scripture says, "Love covereth all sins" (Proverbs 10: 12).

However, blind love can get you "covered" up in a dirty grave. There are many people (far too many to name here) maimed, molested and even murdered as a consequence of love or more accurate, lust.

Notice a difference between the two words. Lust says, if I can't have you nobody can. So I would rather see you dead, than see you with another. Lust is a dangerous thing. However, Love says, if I can't make you happy, maybe someone else can. An old saying goes like this, "If you love somebody, let them go and if they return to you, then it was meant to be."

Biblical love is real love. Paul says, "Love is kind. Love does not behave itself unseemly, seeketh not her own, is not easily provoked and thinketh no evil" (I Cor. 13: 4-5). It would be wise for the young people in relationships today to consider the difference.

Like many in the world today, Geraldine Jones was portrayed as a woman with a bad case of lust, not love. The bible says, "The flesh lusteth against the Spirit" (Gal. 5: 17 KJV). Jesus went further and handcuffed the hands of lust and the Devil together. He said, "Ye are of your Father the devil, and the lusts of your father ye will do" (John 8: 44 KJV).

So Geraldine Jones' reliance on the phrase, "the Devil made me do it" played right into the hands of the Devil. So it is today, the phrase has been used so much now that it has become prevalent jargon in American culture.

Additionally, above and beyond the coining of the phrase, Ms. Jones had some other character flaws that helped set the scene for the phrase' arrival.

My recollection of the television series was this; first, it portrayed Geraldine Jones as a non-spiritual, immoral and un-ethical person. The phrase was but a revelation of her inner spirit and belief system about the Devil. Second, the television series portrayed her as a woman that used whatever or whomever she could as an escape-goat, I meant scapegoat (sorry for the slip up) for her irresponsible behavior. However, her objective was to escape her unpleasant predicament.

For Geraldine Jones, the existence of a Devil was convenient: A convenience used whenever life seemed overwhelming, complicated or demanding. A convenience used when the "going got tough," she got going. Take the easy way out and "by any means necessary" (Malcolm X) was her strategy of life.

Third, Ms. Jones was portrayed as a non-conscientious personality whose comfort zone was satisfied when others received the blame for her failures and shortcomings. While standing alone with no one else around to blame and refusing to accept blame herself, Ms. Jones blamed the Devil. But really, **Did The Devil Make Her Do It?**

Unfortunately, Geraldine Jones did not play the "Blame Game" by herself. Every day, there are countless numbers of human beings, both men and women signing up to play the "blame game." Instead of accepting responsibility for their actions, their number one reaction when accused is to blame someone else. The number two reaction (when number one reaction doesn't work) is to blame the devil as did Geraldine Jones.

Herein lies another lesson that will be well to learn: The pointlessness of playing the "Blame Game." However, pointless, the playing of the "Blame Game" seems second nature to man. It is as old as man himself and dates back to his creation in the Garden of Eden. The third chapter of Genesis detailed the scene.

After the first sin ("eating of the forbidden fruit," fig, not apple, Genesis 3: 7), "God asked Adam, Hast thou eaten of the tree whereof I commanded thee that thou shouldest not eat? And the man said, the woman that thou gavest to be with me, she gave me of the tree and I did eat. And the Lord said unto the woman, what is this that thou hast done? And the woman said, the serpent (Devil) beguiled me and I did eat" (Gen. 3: 12-13 KJV).

Yet, notice God's reaction to their attempted diversion. He did not excuse them from the responsibility of their sin. Neither did their attempt to play the "Blame Game" ease their punishment. In fact, it needs noting (if for no other reason than Scripture accuracy, since debates are still taking place over the woman's (Eve) participation); God handed down five sentences of punishment.

To the woman, three sentences of punishment and two sentences to the man. They are as follows: To the woman God sentenced her to death (1), pain in child birth (2) and the third was subjection to the ruler-ship of her husband (Genesis 3: 16).

To the man God's punishment included death as well, but also, to work by the sweat of his brow (Genesis 3: 19). Clearly, Eve received the greater sentence of punishment. Exegesis revealed the fact that it was due to her initiation of the sin: The Bible says, "She took of the fruit thereof, and did eat, and gave also unto her husband with her; and he did eat" (Genesis 3: 6 KJV).

Yet to no avail, Adam tried to blame both God and Eve. Adam said, "The woman that thou (God) gave to be with me, she gave me of the tree and I did eat." In other words, it's either your fault or hers, but it's surely not mine. Make note, the Blame Game did not work for Adam and did not work for Eve. Every man, woman, boy and girl needs to know that at the Great Day of Judgment, it will not work then, either.

John, the apostle showed a preview of that movie, entitled, **Judgment at the End of Time**. John said, "And I saw the dead, great and small, standing before the throne, and the books were opened. Another book was opened, which is the book of life. The dead were judged out of those things according to what they had done as recorded in the books.

The sea gave up the dead that were in it, and death and Hades gave up the dead that were in them, and each person was judged according to what he had done. Then death and Hades were thrown into the lake of fire. The lake of fire is the second death. If anyone's name was not found written in the book of life, he was thrown into the lake of fire" (Rev. 20: 12-15 NIV).

Therefore, excuses and blame are not tolerated by God. In the garden, Eve was questioned by God and unlike Adam she did not attempt to blame God. Neither did she try and rewind the tape of their conversation like Adam.

One of the possible reasons for her different approach was that there is no written record of a conversation between God and Eve concerning anything: Particularly not about Adam or the Tree of the Knowledge of Good and Evil. Although it's clear that Eve knew the facts concerning the commands that God gave Adam because she stated them to the Serpent.

The only possible scapegoat for Eve was to blame the Devil. So she took the chance and used her only option and blamed him: As did Geraldine Jones. Eve said, "The serpent beguiled me and I did eat" (Gen. 3: 13 KJV).

It is significant to note the actions taken by God surrounding the "Fall of Mankind." First, God punished Eve more severely than Adam. But Adam did not go un-punished. He was severely punished. He now has to go out work by the sweat of his brow, where once he could just lay back and chill out (that was a serious and severe sentence).

Also, God punished the Serpent for his participation as well. He was cursed to crawl upon his belly and enmity was placed between the serpent and his seed and the woman and her seed.

In fact, the woman's seed (Jesus) would bruise the head of the serpent's seed (Satan). There were many lessons learned from the "Fall of man." One of them was the futileness of trying to blame somebody else for our bad behavior. Another lesson learned was: To not make excuses and be satisfied with what God gave us. Somebody said, **"What we are is God's gift to us; how we use it, is our Gift to God."**

However, history, logic and experience suggest that there are two main reasons that millions of men and women blame the Devil. They are as follows: *First,* they blame him because he is an easy target. He is an easy scapegoat. It's easy to blame the Devil.

It's easy to blame him because he has a history of wickedness, lying and stirring things up. In fact, his purpose for existence is evil. (There will be more discussion on his origin and purpose later in chapter III, entitled, who is the Devil?).

The Devil is easy to blame because it is a known fact that whatever the evil of which he is accused, all agree that he possesses the threefold characteristics of guilt to commit the crime. The judicial system prescribes three characteristics to make people prime suspects. The characteristics are motive, opportunity and capability.

First: motive. Jesus told Simon Peter, "Behold, Satan desires to have you that he may sift you as wheat" (Luke 22: 31 KJV). The Devil's motive is to destroy mankind: Make no mistake about it, since Satan's defeat in heaven, his mission in the earth is for that reason and that reason only.

Second: opportunity. Peter says, "Be sober, be vigilant; because your adversary the devil, as a roaring lion, walketh about, seeking whom he may devour (I Peter 5: 8 KJV): Additionally, in the book of Job, Satan responds to God's question of "Whence cometh thou Satan? Satan said, from going to and fro in the earth and walking up and down in it" (Job 1: 7 KJV). Satan is in the earth constantly, and therefore has vast opportunities for destruction.

Third: capability. Capability is defined twofold: Number one, in terms of mental ability or *Will*. Number two: in terms of power and force. The Scripture describes the Devil having both qualities. The mental *will* and reason for doing what he does. Jesus said, "The thief comest not, but for to steal, and kill and to destroy (John 10: 10 KJV):

Additionally, Satan has the power and force as revealed in the gospel of Luke. Jesus said to Simon Peter, "Satan has desired to have you that he may sift (breakdown and destroy) you as wheat (Luke 22: 31 KJV). Satan has the capability. In conclusion, motive, opportunity and capability make the Devil an easy target for blame.

The second reason that he is an easy target for blame is his invisibility. Paul informed man of Satan and the demonic force's invisibility. He said, "We wrestle not against flesh and blood, but against principalities and powers, against the rulers of the darkness of the world, against spiritual wickedness in high places" (Eph. 6: 12 KJV). The fact that he is invisible to the naked eye is crucial to his participation in the maneuvering of evil.

Make note: the Devil will not be seen committing murder. He will not be seen stealing. He will not be seen participating in destructive behavior. Look any place you want, around the home, church, work place, town and country; there will not be any physical evidence tying the Devil to the scene of any crime. You will not see his participation, nor his presence.

Yet, the Scripture repeatedly declares his involvement. Once again, Peter said, "The Devil goest about, seeking whom he may devour" (I Peter 5: 8 KJV). Jesus said, "he is a thief, that comest for to steal, kill and to destroy" (John 10: 10 KJV). In the book of Job, Satan personally testified under oath to God that he "goes to and fro in the earth and walks up and down in it" (Job 1: 7 KJV).

The book of Job revealed a great mystery concerning strong winds (maybe even hurricanes and tornadoes). The Bible said Satan sent a great wind (whirl wind; A New Translation of the Bible, Mof) from the wilderness and smote the four corners of the house and it fell upon the young men and they are dead"(Job 1: 19 NKJV).

There should not be any doubt that Satan is involved in the destruction and devastation of mankind. The Scripture emphatically teaches this fact. Luke informs that he inspired Judas Iscariot to betray Jesus (Luke 22: 3 KJV). He was even present at the scene of the crime of Jesus' arrest (Luke 22: 3 KJV). He was the instigator in all of Job's troubles and downfall (Job 1-2).

He stood up against Israel and provoked David to number Israel, which was against God's wishes (I Chron. 21: 1). The Psalm writer said, "Wicked men were set over the people and Satan stood with them" (Psalm 109: 6 NKJV).

"Satan stood against Joshua the priest to resist him and God rebuked Satan" (Zechariah 3: 1-2 KJV). In the wilderness of Jordan (Matt. 4: 1-11) and after leaving Caesarea Philippi (Matt. 16: 23), Satan was present trying to stop Jesus from going to Calvary.

Satan bound a woman for eighteen years (Luke 13: 16). "Ananias and Sapphira allowed Satan to fill their hearts to lie to the Holy Ghost and to keep back part of the money that they should have given to the church" (Acts 5: 3 KJV). Paul said, "His mission was to turn the people from the power of Satan to God" (Acts 26: 18 KJV).

These are but a selected few of the many recorded Scriptures concerning the evil of the Devil against mankind. Others will be examined in the upcoming chapters. Yet, it is crucial for man to acknowledge and accept the fact of the Devil's involvement in mankind's destruction: Whether he appears at the scene personally or directs the demons in conspiracy, he is involved.

One last word before the chapter is closed, there is one other attribute of the Devil that's note worthy. He is a good administrator. He and the demons of damnation are well organized and work closely together.

Again the passage of Matthew 12 speaks out. Jesus said, "Every kingdom divided against itself is brought to desolation; and every city or house divided against itself shall not stand: And if Satan cast out Satan, he is divided against himself; how shall then his kingdom stand" (Matt. 12: 25-26 KJV).

The problem of division is not evident in Satan's domain. Jesus seemed to indicate that Satan knows; "if Satan cast out demons (his own workers) that he is working against himself and a divided house shall not stand." Also this reason could explain why Satan seems to be winning the fight for the world. Satan's organizations seem well organized and together, subsequently evil is having its way in the world.

As it has been and will continue to be pointed out in the book, there is tragedy and devastation on every street corner of American society as well as on every corner of the globe. Satan's success is an indication that the problem of division is not among the rank and file of his combatants.

On the other hand, the problem of division is major among the army of the Lord. Within the Christian community, it is a problem of huge proportion and implications that can no longer be ignored and somehow, must be dealt with. The Christian Church doesn't seem to get it. But, the Devil and the demons of damnation get it and are experiencing victory after victory because of it.

It's been more than six thousand years of Biblical history and yet, God's army still does not understand the principles of cooperation and togetherness. How ironic, the one group that was installed upon the earth for unity and cooperation, is the one that is so divided.

Jesus addressed this issue with the disciples. "One day, James and John came and requested special seats be given them in the kingdom of God. The other ten disciples over heard the conversation and were much displeased with them for their request for special favor.

Jesus said that they were acting like the godless gentiles and this kind of strife would not be among them. For he came not to be great and ministered unto, but to minister and to give his life, a ransom for many" (Mark 9: 35-45 NKJV).

Still, the Christian church does not get it. The importance of cooperation was understood back in the days of the early church; but has long since been lost. It is ironic that the "church" is the organization that's having the most problems getting along with each other. Even today, the "church" does not seem to realize that the battle is not against fellow human beings (no matter what the race, color, creed or denomination).

The fact that the most segregated hour of the week occurs every Sunday morning when the Church (the body of Christ) comes together is a sad testimony of the transforming power of God. A Time magazine article estimated 90 percent of Americans worship primarily with members of their own race or ethnicity.[9]

> The church needs to recognize and correct its error and move toward full integration. By doing this, the church will show the world a true picture of heaven. Here is another irony. Back in the late sixties; it was primarily the church that pushed for the integration of the public school system and yet, the church has not "taken its own medicine."

The church is dishing it out, but can't take it in. There is another old saying in the community that goes like this, "Talk is cheap; it takes money to buy land." In other words, "Don't talk it, if you can't walk it." Also, it is said that "If you try to improve one person by being a good example, you're improving two. If you try to improve someone without being a good example, you won't improve anybody." [10]

It is not a good reflection on the church that "the number one cause of atheism is Christians. Those who proclaim God with their mouths and deny Him with their lifestyles is what an unbelieving world finds simply unbelievable." [11]

For the church to become what Christ created, there are two things needed most: (1) the reorganization and (2) the refocusing of mankind against the demonic forces that roam the earth. Jesus addressed this issue in Mark 9 above and again, Paul addressed it in the letter to the church at Ephesus.

Paul wrote, "For we wrestle not against flesh and blood, but against principalities and powers, against the rulers of the darkness of this world, against spiritual wickedness in high places" (Eph. 6: 12 KJV).

Yet, despite man's knowledge of the facts about segregation, division and the evils of the world influenced by the Devil; his name is not on the solicitor's suspect list. Despite the incriminating evidence, still no APB (All Points Bulletin) is placed on him and no one expects him to be brought in for questioning. He commits serious crimes, but is beyond the contact of the media, law enforcement and the judicial system.

He never appears in an interview on television. Satan is beyond arrest and detention. He cannot be subpoenaed for confession or deny the charges leveled against him. These facts make him an easy target for blame. He can be easily used as an escape-goat for human error and sin.

In fact, I wish that I had thought about the devil when I was a child. Since he could not be found and questioned, I could have blamed him for my mischievousness. As the youngest of nine children, I misbehaved regularly and sometimes broke some things around the house. Instead of blaming my brothers and sisters that led to nowhere, I should have blamed the Devil.

Whereas mother would find and question my siblings and receive their denial, she could not have found the devil and questioned him. Had I told mother, "the Devil made me do it," I could have possibly escaped blame and punishment. Or could I? Would mother have believed, **"the Devil made me do it?"**

Further exploration of the question is necessary. For instance, if the Devil did not make me do it, who did? Did God make me do it or some other entity? Did I make myself do it and if I did, whose influence was I under, if any? These questions will be addressed later in the book. But first, the next question of examination is, "Who is the Devil and what is it that people need to know about him?"

But before moving on to the next chapter, write down at least three tidbits of information learned from the above chapter.

1._____

2._____

3._____

CHAPTER IV

WHO IS THE DEVIL?

PERSONAL PERCEPTIONS OF THE DEVIL!

*"**Train a child in the way he should go, and when he is old he will not turn from it**"(Proverbs 22: 6 NIV).*

My first experience with the name Devil came when I was a little lad, mother and grandmother would bring up the name. Especially when they thought that I was acting badly (of course I never did). But when they thought I was acting up badly, they would say, "The devil's going to get you." At other times they would say, "If you go out of the yard, the Boogey man is going to get you. Or if you stay out too late in the neighborhood, on the way home, the Boogey man's going to get you."

In order to prove to me that there was such a being as the Devil or the Boogey man, when it rained and the sun shone at the same time, they would say to me, "The Devil is beating his wife." Take this glass and place it on the ground and place your ear against it and you will hear the Devil beating his wife. I did as I was instructed and of course I did not hear anything. But they insisted that at some point, they had heard the Devil beating his wife. Since they were adults, I didn't argue with them and just let it go.

I knew that if I argued with them (particularly grand momma); where I did not hear the Devil beating his wife, I might see the Devil get in her and end up (as the young folk say) "get beat down." Back in those days, children did not argue with adults like many of the young do today (at least not in my grand momma's house).

COMMERCIAL BREAK:

When it comes to the training of children, parents need to revisit the old days. The last generation of parents had the respect of children. When children did wrong, they were afraid of the parent being notified. For instance, at school, when the children did wrong, they would plead with the teachers, not to tell the parent. Today, when the child does wrong, the child can not wait to tell the parent of the incident with the teacher. Back in the day, the parent took the side of the responsible adult. Today, the parent takes the side of the irresponsible child.

Back in the day at the church house, I remember seeing children act out. All the parent had to do was just look at the child and immediately they would straighten up. Today, some parents act as if they are afraid to look at the child. When the children acts out and the other people around, look at the parent, it is as if the parent tries to ignore the actions of the child, seemingly hoping that the child will stop on its own.

While other parents in church, scream and yell (holler) at the children to no avail and the children do not change their behavior one iota. Today, there are far too many parents like Rodney Dangerfield, "they can't get any respect." Man need to be reminded that respect is earned not given. In other words, in order to get respect, you have to give it.

Notice this fact, when people had respect for the Bible and the church, there was more respect for parents and people in general: This fact of reality was not accidental. The solution to the family crisis of respect is to return to the teaching of the Bible or Biblical training. The Bible teaches mankind, "Train up a child in the way that he should go: and when he is old, he will not depart from it" (Proverbs 22: 6 KJV).

When a parent allow the children to ignore, disrespect and disobey their instruction, the parent sin (Yes I said sin) by violating the instructions of God. Sin is disobeying God. Not only in Proverbs 22, But in fact, "Samuel said, Hath the LORD as great delight in burnt offerings and sacrifices, as in obeying the voice of the Lord? Behold, to obey is better than sacrifice, and to hearken than the fat of rams" (I Samuel 15: 22 KJV).

It must be remembered that to have good parents in the world, parents must raise good children. Good parents just don't fall out of the sky, but good trained children grow up to be good parents. Poorly trained children grow up to be poor parents. There are no guarantees, but based upon the preponderance of the evidence, it's more likely than not (according to the T.V. Judges).

Sometime ago, the news T.V. program, Sixty Minutes, did a special on the subject of raising children. They focused on a report about some elephants that were out of control on an island in Africa. It was an experiment to see if, or what effect, proper training or mentoring has on the young.

The adult male elephants were removed from the herd. In a matter of years, the young male elephants were out of control and terrorizing the other animals of the island. The people in charge of the experiment replaced the male adult elephants and within a short period of time, the young elephants were once again under control. Could these elephants have been the source of the African Proverb, "It takes a whole Village to raise a child?"

The message of the experiment was clear, proper training for the young is a necessity. Children need authority figures in their lives. I sat on the DJJ board of South Carolina for six years and I saw first hand the importance of the male authority figure in the home. Sadly, a great number of male juveniles had no father figure in their lives. If the male authority figure was a necessity for the lower animals, it is for the higher animals as well.

While on the subject; the Lord has a word for parents, "Not to provoke the children" (Eph. 6: 4 KJV). Don't harass and do things just to irritate them. "But bring them up in the nurture and admonition (Christian discipline and instruction) of the Lord." Remember "Jesus said, Suffer little children, and forbid them not, to come unto me: for of such is the kingdom of heaven" (Matt. 19: 14KJV). Indeed, children are precious in Jesus' sight.

The song writer said, "Jesus loves the little children, all the children of the world; Red and yellow, Black and White, They are precious in his sight; Jesus loves the little children of the world." Again note what Matthew 18; says, "At the same time came the disciples unto Jesus, saying, who is the greatest in the kingdom of heaven? And Jesus called a little child unto him, and set him in the midst of them: And said, Verily I say unto you, Except ye be converted, and become as little children, ye shall not enter into the kingdom of heaven.

Whosoever therefore shall humble himself as this little child, the same is greatest in the kingdom of heaven. And whosoever shall receive one such little child in my name receiveth me. But whosoever shall offend one of these little ones which believe in me, it was better for him that a millstone were hanged about his neck, and that he were drowned in the depth of the sea" (Matt. 18: 1-6 KJV). Parents and people; be careful with the children.

A reminder to the children: "Children obey your parents in the Lord: for this is right. Honor thy father and thy mother; which is the first commandment with promise (the assurance of a future blessing); that it may be well with thee, and thou mayest live long on the earth" (Eph. 6: 1-3 KJV).

I believe every man, woman, boy and girl alive wants to live long, happy and productive lives. God told man how to accomplish this: "Honor thy father and thy mother; that it may be well with thee."

Moreover, there are other reasons for honoring God's words in the home environment. Think about it, within the earlier chapters of the book, each person named for murder and the other criminal behavior (either nationally or locally) grew up under the guidance of some parent or adult. "They grew up," but apparently something went wrong in their upbringing.

While I realize that parents are not to blame every time a child goes astray, but at least, for the sake of parenthood, it must be acknowledged that the child missed something that he/she needed. The last time I looked at the issue, it was not normal to raise mass murderers and killers. So, something; somewhere went wrong in these people's lives.

Additionally, the high rate of serious crime is a new phenomenon in today's society. No longer can it be denied, something is different about the modern child. Possibly, it could be the lack of training or more specifically, Biblical training.

I think it's safe to say that there is not one person alive, that truly thinks children today are better (or even equal) in character to those in yester years. For one thing, back in the days of my youth, the old folk took raising children to heart: Clearly this is lacking in many homes today.

There are many other things lacking: For instance, the communication between parents and children. Parents need to discuss with their children the consequences of their actions. Example: teenage pregnancy. To eliminate teenage pregnancy, at early ages, parents must communicate with the children.

They must inform them that the Bible teaches that the body is a temple of the Holy Ghost and should not be used for sexual pleasure outside the bounds of Biblical marriage; between a man and woman. In fact, Paul said, "Marriage is honourable in all, and the bed undefiled: but whoremongers and adulterers God will judge" (Hebrews 13: 4 KJV). Parents must inform the children and mean what they say, that if they become pregnant or impregnate others, it will be their responsibility to support and raise the child.

There are too many grand parents raising children in the place of momma and daddy. Love the grand children, but do not allow the parent to abandon their God given responsibility. Make sure the parent knows that the child is their responsibility. Take my word for it, if you alleviate them of their responsibility; prepare to raise the next child and the next one too.

Remember, God commanded the children of Israel to teach the children the word of God. "These commandments that I give you today are to be upon your hearts. Impress them on your children. Talk about them when you sit at home and when you walk along the road, when you lie down and when you get up. Tie them as symbols on your hands and bind them on your foreheads. Write them on the doorframes of your houses and on your gates." (Deut. 6: 6-9 NIV).

I believe that God still knows what's best for the family. As I believe, "the family that prays together; stays together." Job knew this and prayed regularly for his family (Job 1: 5). Unfortunately so does the Devil. When reading the book of Job, note how the Devil feels about the family. He attacked Job's family back then and is attacking yours and mine today. He killed Job's seven sons and three daughters.

Food for thought: there are two intriguing statements recorded in the book of Job dealing with tragedy. In Satan's assault on Job, the first one is found in Job, 1: 16. "The fire of God fell from heaven and burned up the sheep and the servants, and consumed them" (Job 1: 16 NRSV).

It is stated that Satan cause fire to fall from heaven to burn up the fields of sheep along with the servants. The second intriguing statement is found in Job 1: 19. I have briefly mentioned it earlier in the book. But to make the point absolutely clear, allow me to refer to it again.

"A great wind (Whirl wind: B. E. R. Bible) came and smote the house, killing all of Job's seven sons and three daughters. These Biblical accounts raises an interesting question: **Considering the natural disasters occurring around the world and particular the lightening bolts that are igniting fires in California and other places; could Satan have something to do with the ignition of these disastrous fires; or these horrific hurricanes and terrible tornadoes?** It's just submitted as food for thought because he played a part, recorded in the book of Job.

However, it is a fact that the Devil destroyed Job's family and for all practical purposes; destroyed Job's relationship with his wife as well. "His wife said to him, "Are you still holding on to your integrity? Curse God and die"" (Job 2: 9 NIV)!

It's interesting to read other's opinions on the subject of the Devil, Job and Mrs. Job. One writer (in defense of Mrs. Job), said, it was out of love and devotion that she said to Job, "curse God and die." She was looking out for Brother Job, only hoping to put him out of his misery.

But, based upon Job's response to her, he did not think so. "He replied, "You are talking like a foolish woman. Shall we accept good from God, and not trouble?" In all this, Job did not sin in what he said" (Job 2: 10 NIV). With love ones like this, who needs enemy?

Paul said, "Now as the church submits to Christ, so also wives should submit to their husbands in everything. Husbands, love your wives, just as Christ loved the church and gave himself up for her" (Eph. 5:24-25 NIV). Remember, Paul said, "Love is patient; love is kind; love is not envious or boastful or arrogant" (I Cor. 13: 4 NRSV).

THE END OF THE COMMERCIAL BREAK AND BACK TO THE MOVIE:

In the good old days, parents and grand parents spent quality time with their children. Like grand momma did for us. She gathered the children around her and more often than not, even preached to us about right and wrong (She was a Holiness preacher.)

Regularly, her sermons dealt with the Devil. She told us that he was a liar and said to us, "Tell the truth and shame the devil." Also, she told us that he was a murderer, false accuser and an abuser. She told us that at the end of the age (the parousia), he and all of his followers were doomed to a hot place called Hell. Actually, the final state of the Devil and his demons will be the Lake of Fire (Rev. 20: 10 KJV). There will more on the subject in the next chapter, entitled, the Biblical Realities of the Devil.

Sometimes however, when grand momma thought that I was getting out of line, she would say to me, "Steve, remember Hell is still hot, Hell is still hot." Not only was this, the first time I heard about the Devil, it was also the first time I heard about the Devil's home called Hell.

As I look back to my childhood, I remember thinking about all of the things that grand momma said about the Devil. However, at the time, it appeared to me that the picture, painted of the Devil by her resembled her in many ways. Don't misunderstand me, normally; grand momma was a sweet, loving and nice old lady. But when rubbed the wrong way, she was a tyrant. And all of the grand children said, Amen.

When upset, she chastised us harshly (she believed in the old proverb, "spare the rod, spoil the child," Proverbs 16: 24 NKJV). She screamed, hollered and seemingly foamed at the mouth, committing (what we thought) was sure murder. Fortunately for us, it turned out not to be murder because no one ever died. But at the time we thought that we would.

Now I know how Job felt. Sometimes if we ran from the whipping, grand momma would come from next door early in the morning. She would catch us without our clothes on. Her anger was intensified because we ran away and because she was fired up; she set our rear ends on fire.

Once, I remember hearing a preacher preach about Job getting beat down and saying, "Naked came I out of my mother's womb and naked shall I return thither" (Job 1: 21 KJV). Every time I hear the message, I remembered grand momma.

At other times, grand momma was a loving and protective force for her family. The people in the community did not mess with Mrs. Virginia Cunningham Henderson. I remember one night, one of my sister's boyfriends **"thought"** that he had caught her getting out of another man's automobile. In his way of thinking, she had to be taught a lesson.

Someway and somehow, my sister managed to out run him to the gate of our house. We all heard her hollowing and screaming as she ran; and so did grand momma. Grand momma came running out of the house with a loaded double barrel shot gun. She aimed it at the young man, preparing to fire. He saw her and almost killed himself running back up the drive way.

Mo-mom (was what her grand children affectionately called her) Henderson was something else. I thank God for momma and grand momma's discipline and love. **Children need both, discipline and love.** I need to say it again; **children need both, discipline and love.**

In fact, we all need both. Most children get the love, but less and less, today are receiving the discipline. Job believed in it and taught it to his children. He said, "Blessed is the man whom God corrects; so do not despise the discipline of the Almighty. For he wounds, but he also binds up; he injures, but his hands also heal" (Job 5: 17-18 NIV).

One of the major disciplines that grand mother in forced with us was about lying. She would not tolerate liars. I understand why, now, because I have trouble with them also. **Lying is a sin.** Listen up young people, **lying is a sin.** My generation knew this, but this one needs to be reminded that **lying is still a sin.**

In fact, John said, "I heard a voice from heaven saying, all liars shall have their part in the lake which burnest with fire and brimstone: which is the second death" (Rev. 21: 8 KJV).

However at times, we thought, grandmother was not taking her own medicine. While whipping us, she told us that each lick hurt her more than it hurt us. Obviously, our thoughts were that she was not telling the truth, for if it hurt her as much as it hurt us, she would stop.

Yet as I grew older, I came to discover that many of the stories told by some of the old folk were not true. Even some told about the Devil were not true as well. Mind you, some were true, but many were not. One such false portrait painted of the Devil by mother, grandmother and others was, he was red with big ears.

It was also painted erroneously that he had a long tail and a pitch fork in his hands. The false ideologies told about the Devil in my youth contributed somewhat to the need for this examination of the Devil or the Boogeyman.

From an instructional point of view, it is not good theology or proper ideology to makeup creatures or false characteristics. There is danger in promoting Santa Claus, the Easter Bunny, the Tooth Fairy and the Stork that delivered babies.

Santa claus and the bunny rabbit are well known imaginary creatures and need no further explanation. However, "The Tooth Fairy is an example of folklore mythology. The fairy gives children a gift (often money) in exchange for a baby tooth when it comes out of the child's mouth.

Children typically leave the tooth under their pillow for the fairy to take while they sleep. The tooth fairy then adds the tooth to a special part of her mythical and ever expanding all-white tooth castle in the sky."[11] In reality, it was the parent that performed all of what was said to be done by the tooth Fairy.

"The idea that the stork brings babies to waiting parents seems to have its origins with the European white stork in Germany. This stork population would often return to villages from migration at the time of year that many babies were traditionally born." [11] When asked by children where do babies come from, many parents took the easy way out and told their children, the stork brought the babies to their home.

By telling the children these myths, parents may be setting them up for disappointment and distrust. Eventually the truth will emerge and the young people's trust and belief system, particularly in parents could be severely damaged. Children need the security of trust in their parents. "Everyone agrees that trust is essential for decent human relationships."[12]

Theologically, speaking, there is a danger as well. Whenever Santa Claus, the Easter bunny, the tooth Fairy and the Stork that delivers babies turn out to be imaginary creatures; some of the young might think that Satan and God are as well.

The confusion could be disastrous to their need to come to Christ for salvation. Parents need to be careful. My suggestion is, always tell the truth, the whole truth and nothing but the truth, so help us God. Both God and Satan (the Devil, that Old Serpent or whatever, he's called) are real. Stay tuned for chapter IV, "Who Really is the Devil?" (The Biblical Realities of the Devil.)

But before moving on to the next chapter, write down at least three tidbits of information learned from the above chapter.

1._____

2._____

3._____

CHAPTER V

WHO REALLY IS THE DEVIL?

THE BIBLICAL REALITIES OF THE DEVIL!

"My people are destroyed for a lack of knowledge" (Hosea 4: 6 KJV). "And ye shall know the truth and the truth shall make ye free" (John 8: 32 KJV).

The main discussion of the last chapter centered around people's personal perceptions of the Devil. We now move to discuss the Biblical Realities of the Devil or what the Bible says about the Devil. First, notice that God, the Father, said to Hosea, "My people are destroyed for a lack of knowledge" (Hosea 4: 6 KJV). Second, notice that God, the Son (Jesus) said to the Jews that followed him, "And ye shall know the truth and the truth shall make ye free" (John 8: 32 KJV).

Obviously, knowledge is the first step to solving problems. The author of American Educator's "Inflexible Knowledge: The First Step to Expertise" supports this fact.[15]The same is true for man in his dealings with the Devil: Knowledge is the key. Let's explore what man's knowledge of the Devil consist of. "The King James Version translation of the word, "Devil" from the Greek language is dia'bolos; meaning slanderer; one of the principle titles of Satan.

Another translation for Satan (Devil) is Adversary, the archenemy of God and man. Adversary is the most frequently used name for the Devil in the New Testament and appears over fifty times. Devil or slanderer is used over thirty times. Satan, the Devil; Adversary is opposed to all that is good. His character is vile and evil and portrayed as the great deceiver." [9]

A. The origin of Satan (Devil) and Where did he come from?

In response to the question of the origin of the Devil, be reminded first that Colossians 1: 16 says, "For by him (God) were all things created, that are in heaven and are in the earth, visible and invisible, whether they be thrones, or dominions, or principalities or powers: all things were created by Him and for Him."

Second, Proverb 16: 4, Solomon said, 'The Lord has made all things for Himself: Yea, even the wicked for the day of evil." In the book of Isaiah, God said, "I make peace and create evil: I the Lord do these things" (Isaiah 45: 7 KJV).

From the above passages, there's one thing that is crystal clear, "all things were created by God." When I say all things; that is exactly what I mean, all things. Note: The God who created all things is love and holy and desires such personalities surrounding him to be like him. (God will be discussed later, in more detail within Chapter V.)

Yet in summarizing the answer to the question, where did the Devil come from? The Colossian passage informs us that God created all things, including evil and wickedness, which mean, he also created the Devil. Although as has been stated, when God created the Devil, he was not the Devil as we know him today.

Once again for clarity, he was Lucifer, the arch-angel of God. This was before iniquity was found in his heart. Notice real carefully the following passages for the closest explanation found from Biblical exegetical research on the Devil's origin are recorded within the pages of Isaiah, 14: 12-20 and Ezekiel 28: 12-19.

THE PROPOSITION OF ISAIAH!

"How you are fallen from heaven, O Lucifer, son of the morning! How you are cut down to the ground: You who weakened the nations! For you have said in your heart: I will ascend up to heaven, I will exalt my throne above the stars of God; I will also sit on the mount of the congregation, on the farthest sides of the north: I will ascend above the heights of the clouds; *I will be like the most high*" (Isaiah 14: 12-14 NKJV).

THE RESULTS OF LUCIFER'S (DEVIL) SIN!

"Yet you shall be brought down to Sheol (Hell), to the lowest depths of the pit' (Rev. 20: 10). Those who see you will gaze at you, and consider you, saying: Is this the man that made the earth tremble, who shook kingdoms, Who made the world as a wilderness and destroyed its cities, who did not open the house of his prisoners?

And all the kings of the nation, all of them sleep in glory, everyone in his own house; But you are cast out of your grave, like an abominable branch, Like the garment of those who are slain, Thrust through with a sword, who goes down to the stones of the pit, like a corpse trodden under foot.

You will not be joined with them in burial, because you destroyed your land and slain your people. The brood of evil doers shall never be named" (Isaiah 14: 15-20 NKJV).

Before the exegetical process continues, note that scholars assert the words of both Ezekiel 28 and Isaiah 14 to be about Lucifer (Devil). Ezekiel says, "Son of man, take up lamentation for the King of Tyre and say unto him, thus, saith the Lord God: You were the seal of perfection, full of wisdom and perfect in beauty.

You were in Eden, the garden of God; every precious stone was your covering: The sardius, topaz, and diamond, beryl, onyx and jasper, Sapphire, turquoise and emerald with gold. The workmanship of your timbrels and pipes was prepared for you on the day you were created.

You were the anointed cherub who covers; I established you: You were on the holy mountain of God; You walked back and forth in the midst of fiery stones. You were perfect in your ways from the day you were created, till iniquity was found in you. By the abundance of your trading, you became filled with violence within, and you sinned.

Therefore I cast you out as a profane thing, Out of the mountain of God; And I destroyed you, O covering cherub, from the midst of the fiery stones. Your heart was lifted up because of your beauty; You corrupted your way because of your splendor; I cast you to the ground. I laid you before kings that they might gaze at you.

You defiled your sanctuaries, by the multitude of your iniquities, By the iniquity of your trading; Therefore I brought fire from your midst; it devoured you. And I turned you to ashes upon the earth in the sight of all who saw you. All who knew you among the people are astonished at you: You have become a horror, And shall be no more forever" (Ezekiel 28: 12-19 NKJV).

"It must be understood that the writings from both Isaiah and Ezekiel could not refer to any mere mortal human being. Apparently God first peopled the universe or at least certain portions of it with a hierarchy of holy angels, of whom one of the highest orders was (or at least contained) the cherubim. One of them, perhaps the highest of all was "the anointed cherub that covereth," who was created beautiful and perfect in his ways.

This cherub knew that he was beautiful (which required only intelligence), but pride entered his heart and the first sin in the whole history of eternity occurred. Pride led to self-will (Isa. 14: 13-14 KJV) and self-will to rebellion.

This great cherub was named Lucifer and because of his beauty, he rebelled against God. He was cast down from God's throne and became the Adversary (Satan) of God and led other angels into rebellion with him.

Jude 6 says, "And the angels who did not keep their proper domain, but left their own abode, he has now reserved in everlasting chains under darkness for the judgment of the great day." II Peter 2: 4, says, "If God did not spare the angels who sinned, but cast them down to Hell and delivered them into chains of darkness, to be reserved for judgment" (II Peter 2: 4 NKJV). [10]

Note real carefully the sequence of evil and man's sin. In the book of Genesis, the Bible declares, "In the beginning, God created the heaven and the earth. And the earth was without form and void; and darkness was upon the face of the deep." He called forth the light and made the firmament, grass, herbs, and fish of the sea, fowls of the air and cattle of the earth. God saw that it was good.

Everything God made was good. After the completion of the lower creatures, on the sixth day of creation, God created man. He made man in his image and likeness. Let them have dominion over the fish in the sea, the fowl of the air, and over the cattle, over all of the earth and the creeping thing that creeps upon the earth" (Genesis 1: 1-26 NKJV). There was nothing before God created it.

Yet notice, before the man sinned; evil was already in existence. Remember God said to man, "eat of every tree, but the tree of the knowledge of good and evil; do not touch it." Therefore, evil was here before the "Fall" and not brought on by it. (There will be more on the subject of man in chapter VI of the book.)

Moreover, "man was created and created innocent, but with the possibility of becoming holy: The condition being, obedience. But because Satan hated God already, he hated man whom God loved and tried to destroy him." [14] Thus as Genesis three records, the Devil used craftiness and cunning to accomplish the task of mankind's destruction.

B. What the Bible says about the Devil's craftiness and cunning.

Genesis, the first book of the Bible, first introduced the Devil and revealed his deceitful activity. It states, "The serpent (Devil, Satan, according to Revelation 20: 2 KJV) was more subtil (crafty and cunning) than any beast of the field that the Lord God had made" (Gen. 3: 1; KJV).

The Scripture of Revelation 20: 2 was inserted to clarify the thought by many that the Serpent and the Devil are not the same (the Bible declares that they are). The conversation between the serpent and the woman, Eve, revealed the Devil's subtlety.

In fact, the Bible repeatedly issued warning after warning about the Devil's cunning and craftiness. But no one seemed to be listening. II Cor. 2: 11 (KJV), Paul said, "Lest Satan should take advantage of us: for we are not ignorant of his devices."

Ephesians 6: 11(KJV), Paul said, "To put on the whole armor of God that you may be able to stand against the wiles (strategies or cunning) of the devil." In II Corinthians 11: 3 (KJV), Paul said, "But I am afraid that as the serpent deceived Eve by its cunning, your thoughts will be led astray from a sincere and pure devotion to Christ."

Closely read the Genesis passage (Genesis 3: 1) where the Bible introduced the serpent (Devil) to man. Note: he deceived the woman (who ate and gave to the man) intending to destroy them both. They both, the woman and the man, were conned into participating in the most catastrophic event of history: "eating of the forbidden fruit" and thus disobeying God.

The book of Genesis went in great detail, outlining the facts and figures of the event. The book specifically notes that the Serpent (Devil) told Eve that she would not die and that she would be as a god, if she ate from the forbidden fruit. The consequences of the con job by the Devil, though, thousands of years have passed, still haunts men and women today.

The Devil's action of deception brought death; disease, pain, suffering, sorrow and much more of the same into the arena of mankind existence and with every day that pass thousands of human beings meet the fate of death. We hold this truth to be self-evident that Satan is a murderer and a cold-blooded killer.

But not only a murderer, he is a mass murderer. For centuries, he has killed millions of people and so far walked away Scott-free (See Revelation 20).

Although sad, but nevertheless true and the report of Jesus confirmed it. Jesus words, as recorded by John, "Ye are of your father the devil and the lusts of your father ye will do. He was a murderer from the beginning and abode not in the truth because there is no truth in him" (John 8: 44 KJV).

Think about it, a murderer that eludes investigation and kills humans every day. He stalks the world's communities. Man's ignorance and naivety are key weapons in the Devil's arsenal for attacking and murdering mankind. While mankind looks for danger in one direction, Satan sends it from another. He just doesn't kill; he mutilates, maims and mocks.

Satan is the most dangerous serial killer the world has ever known. Even that does not fully describe his devastation and a fact that's even more sad, he's still on the loose, lurking and "seeking whom he may devour" (I Peter 5: 8 KJV).

He shows no mercy because he has none. Even his non-discrimination is a negative. He is an equal opportunist: killing men, women, boys and girls: Killing Black, White, Yellow and Brown: Killing the young and the old. He relies on man's ignorance and un-suspicion as his personal assistants in his genocidal quest.

If Satan was a human being, his face would be on police sketches posted in the banks and post offices. Our doors would be locked and the children never be let out of our sight. There would marches made on the police stations with demands that the authorities patrol the streets twenty four seven.

There would be hot lines set up for tips on the whereabouts of the mad man running wild through our cities. If Satan was a human with a reputation such as his; he would most certainly be on the FBI's most wanted list. America's Most Wanted would feature him weekly. A murderer of such devastation would never be ignored, forgotten or excused.

In fact, Satan should not receive any preferential treatment today. It should be remembered that every time a parent, child or sibling is taken to the graveyard, Satan's deception in the Garden of Eden is the cause. I don't know what that memory does to you, but it brings tears to my eyes.

The thought of the lost of everlasting life: an eternal life without pain, suffering and sorrow: The thought of the lost of a loving mother and a providing father that didn't even have to be: The thought of the loss of children that many parents, suffered through. It was sad for Adam and Eve, but, sickening for you and me.

Yet, it needs reemphasizing that at any time, God could have destroyed Satan. But for His own purpose, He did not. Paul said in Romans 16, "And the God of peace shall bruise Satan under your feet shortly" (Romans 16: 20 KJV). More specifically, the book of Revelation, chapters, 19-20, detailed God's eventual binding of the Devil. First, after the battle of Armageddon, he will be bound for a thousand years in the Millennium (Revelation 20: 3).

After which, he will be loosed for a season and finally, after the battle of Gog and Magog; he will be cast into the Lake of fire for eternity (Revelation 20: 7-8). But until then, God for his own Purpose and Will, allows Satan to run loose in the world. Once again, the book of Proverbs gives evidence of this fact. Wise old Solomon said, "The Lord created all things for himself, yea, even the wicked for the day of evil" (Proverbs 16: 4 KJV).

The prophet Isaiah further verified, even clarified God's position. God said, "I am the Lord and there is none else, there is no God beside me: I girded thee, though thou hast not known me: That they may know from the rising of the sun, and from the west, that there is none beside me. I am the Lord and there is none else. I form the light and create darkness: I make peace and create evil: I, the Lord do all these things" (Isaiah 45: 5-7 KJV).

Both in the past and present, God used the Devil to test man's love and loyalty with evil (Job 1-2). God's hope for man remains undaunted that man would prove worthy of His love, trust and provision. The question has been asked a thousand times by believers, why did God create evil? Or better yet, why does He allow evil and the Devil to continue its reign of destruction?

Biblical exegesis reveals only one answer: God wanted man to have a choice and use the choice for God, without reservation, hesitation or intimidation. As human beings created in his image and likeness (Genesis 1:26), we value love greater when it is given freely to us.

The Beatles had a song entitled, "Money can't buy me love. Money can buy diamond rings; money can buy all sorts of things. But I don't care too much for money because money can't buy me love." God accepts no less than love given freely from man.

In the Garden of Eden, Adam and Eve failed to choose God and allowed the Serpent (Devil) to influence them into disobedience. But in the wilderness of Jordan, Jesus succeeded and fulfilled the hope that God had for man.

Today, God is still looking for men and women to fulfill His *will* by obeying His voice. Matthew 4: 1 unveils the scene of Jesus' (the Second

Adam's) victory: "Then was Jesus led up of the Spirit into the wilderness to be tempted of the Devil."

Please note that the Spirit of the Lord led Jesus into the wilderness to be tempted of the Devil. God led Him to the temptation with the intent for him to take advantage of the opportunity to overcome and bless the name of God.

Yes, it is true that sometimes God leads man to the temptation. Yet, when He does, God leads him there for him (man) to succeed. On the other hand, when the Devil leads man to the temptation, he leads him there to fail and fall. The success or failure depends upon man's source of information. If he listens to public opinion and his own knowledge, he fails. But if he listens to the Word of God, he succeeds.

Please, note the difference. Solomon reminds man to, "Trust in the LORD with all your heart and lean not on your own understanding; in all your ways acknowledge him, and he will make your paths straight. Do not be wise in your own eyes; fear the LORD and shun evil" (Proverb 3: 5-7 NIV).

Matthew's Gospel says, "And when he had fasted forty days and forty nights, afterwards he was hungry" (Matt. 4: 2 KJV). The Devil knows much about man's condition. The text points out that he knew the point of Jesus' weakest state. The Devil and the demons are aware of you and me. It is imperative that we acknowledge his determination and perseverance to cause us pain and suffering.

The Scripture says, "When the tempter came to him, he said, if you are the Son of God, command that these stones be made bread" (Matt. 4: 3 KJV).

Once again, Satan tried to cast doubt into the mind of Jesus in hope of getting Him to try and prove his identity. A tactic used by him on mankind for the last six thousands years. In fact, it was the first and the same tactic he used on Adam and Eve back in the Garden of Eden (Genesis 3: 1-5 NKJV).

The Serpent (Satan) told Eve, God knows who you are and what you are capable of becoming, a god, that's why he doesn't want you to eat from the Tree of the knowledge of good and evil. Eve was an easy sell on the idea of eating and becoming a god because she wanted God-like power. She wanted to do things her way. She really did not want God and anybody else to stand in the way of her desires.

Basically Eve wanted Self-Determination where she could determine her own consequences instead of another. However, this is one of the attributes of the Almighty God. Yet, mankind still has the same conflict, even as this book is being read: There is a conflict between self rule and God rule.

Everyday man faces the conflict of having to choose, do I tithe to God or do I keep the money for myself? Do I get dressed and drive myself to the church or do I rest and relax? Do I do this for me or do I do that for God and others? The examples are long and in-exhaustive. But in short, the question of consequence is; do I give in to the lusts of the flesh, or to the "words that proceed out of the mouth of God" (Matt. 4: 4 KJV)?

Also, "Jesus replied: "'Love the Lord your God with all your heart and with all your soul and with all your mind.' This is the first and greatest commandment. And the second is like it: 'Love your neighbor as yourself.' All the Law and the Prophets hang on these two commandments" (Matt. 22: 37-40 NIV).

Obviously, the Devil wants you to give in to the desires of the flesh. The Devil knows that when you give in to the desires of the flesh and withhold your tithes and offerings, God will withhold your blessings. Recorded in the book of Malachi, God said to Israel, "Bring the whole tithe into the storehouse, that there may be food in my house.

Test me in this," says the LORD Almighty, "and see if I will not throw open the floodgates of heaven and pour out so much blessing that you will not have room enough for it. I will prevent pests from devouring your crops, and the vines in your fields will not cast their fruit," says the LORD Almighty" (Malachi 3: 10-11 NIV).

The Devil knows that when you stay away from the church worship, you not only miss worship of the Lord, but the fellowship of fellow believers that's necessary for spiritual growth. Paul said. "Let us not give up meeting together, as some are in the habit of doing, but let us encourage one another-and all the more as you see the Day approaching" (Hebrews 10: 25 NIV).

When wrestling with the flesh and the prince of this world (Satan), my recommendation is to consider the methodology of Jesus and withstand the Devil's influence by relying on the Word of God.

"But he answered and said, it is written, man shall not live by bread alone, but by every word that proceeds out of the mouth of God" (Matt. 4: 4 KJV). Mankind is to live by God's commands and instructions if he is to find happiness and fulfillment.

Jesus said, "He that hath my commandments and keepeth them, he it is that loveth me: and he that loveth me shall be loved of my Father, and I will love him and manifest myself unto him" (John 14: 21 KJV). Man needs to be reminded that obedience to the Devil in any form or fashion is disobedience to God and will lead to certain destruction (John 10: 10 KJV).

"Then the Devil took him up into the holy city, set him on the pinnacle of the temple" (the tradition being, the temple at Jerusalem was 180 feet high to its peak.") [16] And said, to him, "If you are the Son of God, throw yourself down, for it is written: he shall give his angels charge over you and in their hands they shall bear you up, lest you dash your foot against a stone" (Matthew 4: 5-6 NKJV).

Again, the lying and deceitful nature of the Devil is revealed. Make note that Devil also knows God's word. The verse, the Devil quoted was from the 91st Psalm. Yet the Devil intentionally misquoted it. The Psalmist said, "He shall give his angels charge over you to keep you in all thy ways" (Psalm 91: 11-12 NKJV). Satan conveniently left out the words, "To keep you in all thy ways," or the ways of God and the angel will bear thee up: A deliberate strategy to misquote the words of God and mislead Jesus.

The commands of Jesus and the advice of the leadership of Christianity are for the people of the world and specifically for the Body of Christ to study the Word of God for themselves. Paul says, "Study to show thyself approved unto God, a workman that needeth not to be ashamed, rightly dividing the word of truth. But shun profane and vain babblings: for they will increase unto more ungodliness" (II Tim. 2: 15-16 KJV).

If there is any hope to defeat the Devil, it has and will always be through the Word of God. For if the Devil has the audacity to attempt to mislead Jesus with the Scripture, man must know that he will tempt us as well. "Jesus said unto him again, "It is written, you shall not tempt the Lord your God" (Matt. 4: 7 KJV).

"Again, the Devil took him up into an exceedingly high mountain and showed him all of the kingdoms of the world and their glory. And he said to Him, "All these things will I give unto you, if you will fall down and worship me" (Matthew 4: 9 NKJV).

Luke's rendering states that Satan offered Jesus all of the power and glory of the kingdom that has been delivered to him" (Luke 4: 6 NKJV). The key difference between Luke and Matthew's version is that Luke indicates the power and glory of the world was given to Satan from somebody, obviously, God.

Allow me the privilege to affirm and confirm the fact that Satan has no power or ownership apart from God; an important reality of theology. The Psalmist declared, "The earth is the Lords and the fullness thereof;

the world and they that dwell therein. For he founded it upon the seas and established it upon the floods" (Psalm 24: 1-2 KJV).

The book of Job also confirms this fact. Satan went to God for permission to attack Job on every occasion. God gave permission, but with direct directions how far the Devil was to go in the attack on Job. In other words, God holds the reigns of the world in the palm of his hands. Rejoice humans, again I say rejoice. God is in charge, not the Devil. There's more on God in chapter five, entitled, Who Is God?

"Then Jesus said to him, away with you Satan! For it is written, "You shall worship the Lord your God and him only you shall serve. Then the Devil left him and behold angels came and ministered to him" (Matthew 4: 10-11 Nor). However, Luke 4: 13 informs us that the "Devil left Jesus only for a season:" Another indication (along with the Job, Peter and other's situation) that the Devil is consistently coming into and going out of man's domain.

Before leaving the temptation of Jesus out in the wilderness of Jordan, there are several key observations that are worth their weight in gold. The temptation followed the same pattern that the Serpent used back in the Garden of Eden. Rick Warren says that Satan always follow the same pattern of temptation. He identified it and labeled it into a four step pattern. It just so happened that all of the components begin with the letter D.

First, he says Satan identifies a "Desire" within the person: A weakness and vulnerability of some kind that he can work with. Satan then creates "Doubt" in God or in God's word. To me, this doubt results in the subject no longer possessing complete confidence, leaving the door opened to insecurity and disbelief.

Once the door of doubt and disbelief are opened, Satan accesses the rooms of Deception. Remember Satan is an expert in the field of cunning and deception. The Bible repeatedly reminds us of Satan's "subtlety" (Gen. 3: 1 & Eph. 6: 11).

Finally, according to Rick Warren; the deception of the Devil leads to the fourth D; Disobedience.[33] Make note that disobedience is the big concern of God. The citing of Mr. Warren's Pattern is to further affirm the main thesis of the book that Satan is behind temptation.

Even more to the point, James said, "Let no man say when he is tempted, I am tempted of God: for God cannot be tempted with evil, neither tempteth he any man: But every man is tempted, when he is drawn away of his own lust, and enticed. Then when lust hath conceived, it bringeth forth sin: and sin, when it is finished, bringeth forth death" (James 1: 13-15 KJV).

To summarize what has been said up to now on the question, "Did the Devil make me do it?" Briefly, let us review the over whelming Scriptural passages related to the subject. The Bible says, "Then, he called his 12 disciples unto him, and gave them power and authority over all devils, and to cure diseases" (Luke 9: 1 KJV). **Mankind has the power over all Devils.**

"And the 70 returned again with joy, saying, Lord, even the devils are subject unto us through thy name. And he said unto them, I beheld Satan as lightening fall from heaven. Behold, I give you power to tread upon serpents and scorpions and over all the power of the enemy: (Luke 10: 17-19a KJV). **Mankind has power over the enemy.**

Jesus said, "Simon, Simon, Satan hath desireth to have you that he may sift you as wheat, but I have prayed for thee" (Luke 22: 31 KJV). **Jesus prayed for mankind to overcome the Devil and God grant's Jesus' prayers.**

Satan said, "But put forth thine hand now, and touch all that he hath, and he will curse thee to thy face. And the LORD said unto Satan, Behold, all that he hath is in thy power; only upon himself put not forth thine hand" (Job 1: 11-12 KJV). **God has Satan under subjection on man's behalf.**

Paul said, "There hath no temptation taken you, such as is common to man: but God is faithful who will not suffer you to be tempted above that ye are able; but with every temptation also make a way to escape, that ye may be able to bear it. Wherefore, my dearly beloved, flee from idolatry" (I Corinth. 10: 13-14 KJV).

With every temptation, there is a way for man to escape. There you have it, the Biblical report is in. Satan CAN NOT do any thing to the child of God without God's permission (Job 1-2).

Therefore, the answer to the question, did the Devil make me do it, is absolutely not: No way and no how: A resounding "no." Let it be proclaimed from the rooftop, the Devil cannot make any person do any thing. The Bible says, "Submit yourselves therefore to God. Resist the devil, and he will flee from you" (James 4: 7 KJV).

Mankind has the power to resist. Thank God, Thank God; Thank God. Therefore, make "temptation a stepping stone rather than a stumbling block. An opportunity rather than an obstacle: A testimony rather than a test: A privilege rather than a protest. Temptation is an opportunity to do right as it is to do wrong. Temptation simply provides the choice." [25] Let us make the right choice; to glorify God and shame the Devil.

Now that the question (did the Devil make me do it), has been thoroughly explored, Biblically analyzed and answered with a resounding no, there are a few other questions remaining that need addressing. Such as, if the Devil did not make me do it, who did? Does God make me do what I do or some other entity? Do I make myself do what I do and if I do, whose influence am I under, if any?

The jury of history has rendered its verdict on the first question with a resounding, no. Now the book moves to its present case on the second question: does God make me do what I do? The next chapter, entitled, "Who is God" will address the question. But first, in summarizing the present chapter, here are some of the Biblical highlights that one should now be conscious of!

The Devil's intentions toward mankind:
A. Jesus said, "The thief comest but for to steal, kill and destroy." (John 10: 10 KJV). The Devil is the thief and his intentions are clear. He wants man broke and busted, dead and lost.

B. Peter said, "Be sober, be vigilant: because your adversary, the Devil, walketh about like a roaring lion, seeking whom he may devour: whom resist steadfast in the faith, knowing that the same afflictions are accomplished in your brethren that are in the world" (I Peter 5: 8-9 KJV).

Peter's instructions to man is to be sober and vigilant. Man can defeat the Devil, but needs to be at his best. "He is at his best when he is watchful, alert and exercises self control." [17]

The reason for this caution, mankind needs to be aware that there is an adversary, called the Devil, lurking. Remember the words of Peter, "He walketh about, like a roaring lion, seeking whom he may devour." In other words, this enemy, like a wild animal is roaming the streets and looking for any person to kill and eat. So man better be aware.

In II Timothy, Paul advised Timothy that "there were some that needed to recover themselves out of the snare of the Devil who were taken captive by him at his will"(II Tim 2: 26). The Devil is not only walking about in the world seeking, but is also setting traps for men and women. Even today, some men and women have fallen victim to the traps set by Satan. Paul warned man about a behind the scene, manipulating Devil.

The Devil's *Will* is clear. It is to take captive (or control of) as many human beings as he desires. Even though Paul warned about it, he also gave hope that man can recover and escape from the captivity of the devil. In other words, when the Devil knocks you down, you don't have to stay down.

Recover, break-loose and escape. Remember "failure is not being knocked down, it's staying down" (Source Unknown). The book of Zechariah informed mankind that "the guiding angel showed Joshua the high priest standing before the angel of the Lord and Satan standing at his right hand ready to oppose him. And the Lord said to Satan, the Lord rebukes you Satan! The Lord who has chosen Jerusalem rebukes you! Is this not a brand plucked from the fire" (Zech. 3: 1-2 NKJV)?

Exegesis reports that Joshua the high priest was preparing to go to battle. The angel of the Lord was there to assist him in the victory. Yet the prophet Zechariah made note that Satan was also there standing with them to resist and oppose their efforts.

Once again, Satan appeared before the angelic host to instigate havoc upon the human family. There should not be any doubt concerning his purpose of destruction. But, thank God for his intervention. He intervened and rebuked Satan. He said, I have decided to have mercy on the city of Jerusalem, Joshua and the nation. Though it was like pulling burning sticks from the fire.

The Devil's influence and control over mankind: Both in the Old Testament and the New Testament, the Devil demonstrated influence and control over man. No one can forget the serpent's (Devil) influence over Adam and Eve in the Garden of Eden (Genesis 3: 1KJV). It has been repeatedly discussed and will not be here, but must be listed. It was by far the most catastrophic event in the history of man and the one with the most long lasting ramifications.

"Satan stood up against Israel to provoke David to number Israel" (I Chron 21: 1-3 KJV). Even though Joab protested for God, David did as Satan inspired. The Devil has a history of provoking and inspiring humans to go against the will of God. Men and women need to be mindful of the agenda of the Devil. Satan doesn't do any thing for the advancement of mankind. You can take that fact to the bank and deposit it.

The book of Job's account verifies Satan's (Devil) mission. God asked him, whence cometh thou Satan? He answered, from going to and fro and up and down in the earth. Eventually, he asked God for permission to bring destruction on Job and his family (Job, chapters 1-2 KJV).

The New Testament records John's words, "And supper being ended, the Devil having already put into the heart of Judas Iscariot, Simon's son to betray him" (John 13:2 NKJV). Further, in the text, John says, "Now, after the piece of bread, Satan entered him. Then Jesus said to him, what you do, do quickly" (John 13: 27 NKJV).

He then having received the sop went immediately out: and it was night (John 13: 30 KJV). The point being that after Satan entered him; he went out and betrayed Jesus to the multitudes.

Physician Luke records Jesus saying, "So ought not this woman, being a daughter of Abraham, whom Satan hath bound-think of it for eighteen years, be loosed on the Sabbath" (Luke 13: 16 NKJV).

Exegesis reveals the woman had an issue of blood for eighteen years. In the eyes of Jesus, sickness was the result of Satan. There are many Scripture passages of sickness that Jesus concluded were the result of Satanic or demonic activity.

Mark five records one such occasion. The demoniac man was crying and cutting himself with stones. Society thought that he was crazy, howbeit; Jesus concluded that he was possessed with unclean spirits. He called them out of the man and sure enough the man was made well (Mark 5: 1-19 NKJV).

"But he turned and said to Peter, "Get thee behind me, Satan! You are an offense to me, for you are not mindful of the things of God, but the things of men" (Matt. 16: 23 NKJV).

"But Peter said, Ananias, why hast Satan fill your heart to lie to the Holy Ghost and keep back part of the price of the land for thyself"(Acts 5: 3 NKJV).

"Be angry and sin not. Do not let the sun go down on your wrath, nor give place to the Devil (Eph. 4: 26-27 KJV).

"In this the children of God and the children of the Devil are manifest: Whosoever does not practice righteousness is not of God, nor is he that does not love his brother (I John 3: 10 NKJV).

"Jesus said, haven't I chosen you 12 and one of you is a devil" (John 6: 70 KJV)?

""In your anger do not sin:" Do not let the sun go down while you are still angry, and do not give the **devil a foothold.** He who has been stealing must steal no longer, but must work, doing something useful with his own hands, that he may have something to share with those in need.

Do not let any unwholesome talk come out of your mouths, but only what is helpful for building others up according to their needs, that it may benefit those who listen. And do not grieve the Holy Spirit of God, with whom you were sealed for the day of redemption" (Eph. 4: 27-30 NIV).

"You are a child of the Devil and an enemy of everything that is right" (Acts 13: 10 KJV).

The Devil's attributes:
It is important to know as much as possible about the Devil in order to recognize him. The importance of this recognition can not be over emphasized. It is a life and death issue. Recognize him in time and live life to the fullest. Fail and allow him to slip up on you and death can result.

Hebrews 2: 10, says, "the Devil had the power of death, but Jesus came to destroy him" (Hebrews 2: 10 NIV).

Sinner
It needs noting that the Devil was the first sinner. In fact, sin began in the Devil and is of the devil. It needs to be recognized that sin came into existence as a result of Lucifer's (Devil) rebellion. John said, "He that sins is of the Devil: for the Devil has sinned from the beginning. For this purpose the Son of God was manifested that he might destroy the works of the Devil" (I John 3: 8 KJV).

Destroyer!
Jesus said to Peter, Simon, Simon, behold Satan desires to have you that he may sift (Grind) you as wheat, but I am praying for you" (Luke 22: 31 KJV).

Peter says, "Be sober: Be vigilant because your adversary the Devil walketh about seeking whom he may devour" (I Peter 5: 8 KJV). Satan said, "But stretch out your hand and strike everything he has, and he will surely curse you to your face" (Job 1: 11 NIV).

Paul said, "God will give them repentance, to the acknowledgment of the truth; and they that come to their senses and escape the snare of the Devil, who are taken captive by him at his will" (I Tim. 2: 25-26 NKJV).

Thief!
"The Thief comest for to steal, kill and to destroy" (John 10: 10 KJV).

Jesus said, "And the enemy that sows them is the Devil; and he comes and steals them away" (Matt. 13: 39 KJV). Satan comes and steals the word of God away from hearers that was sown (Mark 4: 15 KJV).

Satan does not want any one saved. This is a reference to the word of God being planted into the potential believer. Satan makes an attempt to snatch up the word before it sinks into the believer's heart: Once again revealing the Devil's activity to interfere with the salvation of mankind.

Con Artist!
"Now the serpent was more crafty than any of the wild animals the LORD God had made" (Gen. 3: 1 NIV).

But I am afraid that just as Eve was deceived by the serpent's cunning, your minds may somehow be led astray from your sincere and pure devotion to Christ" (II Cor. 11: 3 NIV). "Put on the full armor of God so that you can take your stand against the devil's schemes. For our struggle is not against flesh and blood, but against the rulers, against the authorities; against the powers of this dark world and against the spiritual forces of evil in the heavenly realms" (Eph. 6: 11-12 NIV).

Full of Pride:
"Not a novice, lest being puffed up with pride, he falls into the same condemnation as the devil" (I Tim. 3: 6 KJV). In the fourth chapter of Matthew, the Devil demonstrated the characteristic of pride. He tried to get Jesus to jump off of the temple in the sight of mankind and allow the angels to sweep him up.

This event would be a grand demonstration to the world of Jesus' power and he would feel great pride and joy. However, let mankind take note and remember Jesus' response, "It is written, Thou shalt not tempt the Lord thy God" (Matt. 4: 7 KJV).

How to avoid the Devil:
"Submit yourselves therefore to God and resist the Devil and he will flee from you" (James 4: 7 NKJV).

"In your anger do not sin:" Do not let the sun go down while you are still angry, and do not give the devil a foothold" (Eph. 4: 27 NIV).

Devil works miracles.
"For they are the spirits of devils, working miracles, which go forth unto the kings of the earth and of the whole world; to gather them to the battle of that great day of God, Almighty" (Rev 16: 14 KJV).

The final analysis of the chapter entitled, Who Is the Devil," answered only part of the question; did the Devil make me do it? Clearly from all that has been clarified and verified, the answer is NO, the devil did not make man do it. It was demonstrated in the book of Job; and time and time again ever since that the Devil can not make man do anything. Man is under the protective hand of the almighty God.

Yet, there are other questions remaining. Such as, if the Devil did not make me do it, who did? Did God make me do what I did or some other entity? Did I make myself do it and if I did, whose influence was I under, if any?

The first question has been answered. Now the book moves to answer the second question. Does God make me do what I do? This is the question that will be addressed in the next chapter, entitled, who is God?

But before moving on to the next chapter, write down at least three tidbits of information learned from the above chapter.

1._____

2._____

3._____

CHAPTER VI

DOES GOD MAKE ME DO WHAT I DO? WHO IS GOD?

PERSONAL AND BIBLICAL REALITIES OF GOD

"Giving thanks to the Father, who has enabled you to share in the inheritance of the saints in the light. He has rescued us from the power of darkness and transferred us into the kingdom of his beloved Son, in whom we have redemption, the forgiveness of sins. He is the image of the invisible God, the firstborn of all creation; for in him all things in heaven and on earth were created, things visible and invisible, whether thrones or dominions or rulers or powers--all things have been created through him and for him. He himself is before all things, and in him all things hold together" (Colossians 1: 12- 17 NRSV).

Most people's experiences of life in the world usually come from those closest to them. It's no secret that parents have the most influence on their children. The mass amount of research and data on the subject is without dispute.

In fact, the reason that all of my siblings (five boys and three girls) and I only use the facial skin cream, Noxzema, was because our mother

(Mrs. Ola Mae Lomax) and grandmother (Mrs. Virginia Henderson) declared it to be the seventh wonder of the world.

Like I inherited mother's position on Noxzema; I also inherited mother's position on many other things, including God. In chapter two, it was noted that my first experience with the name, Devil came from Momma and Grand Momma's conversations with me.

The first time I heard the name God; it came down the same pathway: from the mind, through the teeth and across the lips of momma and grand momma. (Remember, I am reminiscing as a little boy.)

Now that I am an adult, I am a living witness to the truth of the statement that children are greatly influenced by their parents. As a pastor, I attend church regularly a long with my wife (Frances) and our children. They were brought up in the church.

To further the point that parent's influence their children; my wife's father was a preacher and so he influenced my wife. My wife influenced me, we influenced the children and they influenced theirs, and on and on it goes. The fact that all of my children were regular church attendees, even while away at college is another testimony of the influence, parents possess. Even now, some of our children are married living in other cities, yet every Sunday, they make their way to the church house.

Growing up in the Green Line community of Greenville, South Carolina; there were six boys and three girls living under one roof (in addition to momma). The house was concrete; with three small rooms. At some point, a fourth room was added to the house that we called the living room. The walls of all of the rooms were made of concrete as well. Being an old house, some of the mortar that held the blocks together had fallen out.

The importance of this notation is to unveil the fact that there were few secrets kept within the house. It was known by all that whatever was stated in one room would be heard throughout the house. This missing mortar was important because through those cracks in the walls, I first heard the name, God and Jesus Christ.

Every morning and night, I heard momma talking to these people. At first, I wondered, to whom was she talking? So I sat up and listened. I thought it strange because I never heard anyone answer her questions or respond back to her in any way, shape or form.

Also, I knew the names of every one that lived in the house and since there were ten of us living in a four room house; we knew each other pretty well. Besides, there wasn't any room for visitors to spend the night. So, to hear her calling the names, God, the Father or the Lord, Jesus, Christ opened the ears of my curiosity.

For a long period of time, the conversations with (what I called) the invisible men continued. Many times, I began to ask her about them, but stopped out of fear and respect. I was afraid because I thought; she might accuse me of eavesdropping or being nosey. And in my day, children stayed out grown folk business.

This is another lesson that parents should learn and in force with their children. There are too many parents allowing their children to get involved in grown folks business. There will be grown folks having conversations and children will walk up and stand there listening and sometimes will start participating. Back in the days when children had respect for their elders, parents did not tolerate a child's interference in an adult's conversation.

However, in due time, momma told me all of what she knew about the personalities; God and Jesus Christ. During the conversation, I was greatly relieved because I was beginning to worry about her, talking to people that no one but her could see.

But thank God, mother was all right and I finally came to know who they were. I said who they were, but the correct theology is to say who the Father and Son are, and not who they were: for they are alive and will be forevermore.

However from that point until the present, I heard much about God and Jesus Christ. I even heard that the church building was their house and whenever you needed to find them, go to the church. Although, I must admit that I hardly ever went to the church as a lad. It seems a bit strange now that I did not go, since I was told that when one needed to find God and Christ, the church was the place to go.

As I meditate on the issue, the only logical conclusion that I can make about it is this, I did not go to church because mother did not go. I said earlier that the research and data indicates that children are more influenced by their parents than any other group.

Let me interject a note of wisdom and exhortation, parents please take note of what you tell your children. But more importantly, take note of how you act around them. Many children learn by just watching and listening to the parents. And the parents are unaware that the children are absorbing every action into their systems.

So parents take note of what you do around them. For "Actions speak louder than words:" it's not what you say, it's what you do. Some one once said, "I would rather **see** a sermon any day of the week, than just **hear** one on Sunday."

It is the parent's responsibility to train up their children properly. The Bible says, "Train up a child in the way that he should go: and when he is old, he will not depart from it" (Proverbs 22: 6 KJV).

The six chapter of Deuteronomy, God gave this command to Moses. "These commandments that I give you today are to be upon your hearts. Impress them on your children. Talk about them when you sit at home and when you walk along the road, when you lie down and when you get up" (Deuteronomy 6: 6-7 NIV).

COMMERCIAL BREAK:
SOME THINGS EVERY PERSON NEED TO KNOW ABOUT THE CHURCH!

"Keep watch over yourselves and all the flock of which the Holy Spirit has made you overseers. Be shepherds of the church of God, which He bought with his own blood" (Acts 20: 28 NIV).

Although as stated above; the teaching of God was not mandated to me as I was not a regular church attendee. But, allow me to say that even if a person did not attend church as a child, it is never too late. Somebody said, "It's better late than never."

As I said, I did not attend church regularly, but, I did attend church on Easter Sundays. The new outfits Momma bought us to wear were great incentives.

In fact, I remember one Easter Sunday morning in particular. A friend of mine and I went to the church. We knocked on the door and waited for someone to either open it or say, come in.

Eventually a young girl opened the door and immediately, we thought that this was a fun place to be. The people seemed happy and were laughing as we walked in. I didn't know until much later that the joke was on us for knocking on the church door (Remember I was a child and un-churched).

As such, I was deficient in knowledge and understanding about God and the church. What you don't know, you just don't know. Somebody said, "What you don't know can't hurt you," but as you can see, sometimes it can (but that is another book that I plan to write).

My deficiency in the knowledge of God and the church displayed itself in other ways besides just knocking on the church's doors. Those friends and I that did not go to church had little resistance to the influence of the Devil. We participated in the gang activity that included breaking and entering, theft and other crimes that will be left un-mentioned: but you get the picture.

The morality of God that is taught in the church (even with all of its problems) is critical to the development of people in the Society. The Biblical and social evidence is clear that the breakdown of morality in society is directly related to the lack of church attendance and influence.

What you don't know can hurt you. Parents go to church and take your children with you. Paul warns, "Let us not give up meeting together, as some are in the habit of doing, but let us encourage one another--and all the more as you see the Day approaching " (Hebrews 10: 25 NIV). The church is so important that I need to reiterate a couple of crucial points.

The first and most important is the fact that Jesus built the church and died for it. Jesus said, "And I also say unto thee, that thou art Peter, and upon this rock, I will build my church; and the gates of hell shall not prevail against it" (Matt. 16: 18 KJV).

Paul said, "Keep watch over yourselves and all the flock of which the Holy Spirit has made you overseers. Be shepherds of the church of God, which He bought with his own blood" (Acts 20: 28 NIV).

The second important point is that it is a command to attend church as stated above in Hebrews 10: 25.

The third important point is the members of the church have an obligation to one another to provoke good works and exhort one another" (Hebrews 10: 24 KJV).

The final important point of the church is its benefits to the membership. The book of Acts 2: 42-47 reveals the following benefits:

1. **The first one has to be salvation.** Although salvation is of Christ, it must be listed as the greatest benefit of the church as well.

2. **Instruction** ("Study to show thyself approved unto God, a workman that needeth not to be ashamed, rightly dividing the word of truth" ii Tim 2: 15 KJV).

3. **Fellowship** ("And let us consider how to provoke one another to love and good deeds, not neglecting to meet together, as is the habit of some, but encouraging one another, and all the more as you see the Day approaching" (Hebrews 10: 24-25 NKJV) .

4. **Remembering and Honoring Jesus through the breaking of bread** ("For I received from the Lord what I also handed on to you, that the Lord Jesus on the night when he was betrayed took a loaf of bread, and when he had given thanks, he broke it and said, "This is my body that is for you. Do this in remembrance of me."

   In the same way he took the cup also, after supper, saying, "This cup is the new covenant in my blood. Do this, as often as you drink it, in remembrance of me." For as often as you eat this bread and drink the cup, you proclaim the Lord's death until he comes. Whoever, therefore, eats the bread or drinks the cup of the Lord in an unworthy manner will be answerable for the body and blood of the Lord " I Cor. 11: 23-27 NRSV).

5. **Praying** ("Are any among you suffering? They should pray. Are any cheerful? They should sing songs of praise. Are any among you sick? They should call for the elders of the church and have them pray over them, anointing them with oil in the name of the Lord.

The prayer of faith will save the sick, and the Lord will raise them up; and anyone who has committed sins will be forgiven" (James 5: 13-15 NRSV).

6. **The presence of God.** ("Go therefore and make disciples of all nations, baptizing them in the name of the Father and of the Son and of the Holy Spirit, and teaching them to obey everything that I have commanded you. And remember, I am with you always, to the end of the age" (Matt. 28: 19-20).

7. **Common Cause (Things in common with fellow believers).** "They devoted themselves to the apostles' teaching and fellowship, to the breaking of bread and the prayers. Awe came upon everyone, because many wonders and signs were being done by the apostles.

    All who believed were together and had all things in common" (Acts 2: 42-44 NRSV);

8. **Assistance** ("they would sell their possessions and goods and distribute the proceeds to all, as any had need. Day by day, as they spent much time together in the temple, they broke bread at home and ate their food with glad and generous hearts, praising God and having the goodwill of all the people. And day by day the Lord added to their number those who were being saved" (Acts 2: 45-47 NRSV).

END OF COMMERCIAL BREAK.

There is another reason for the writing of this exegetical work about the Devil; God and man: that it will enhance every reader's knowledge and understanding on the subject. Remember God's words to the prophet Hosea, "My people are destroyed for a lack of knowledge: because thou hast rejected knowledge, I will also reject thee" (Hosea 4: 6 KJV).

So, what should man's knowledge consist of when it comes to God? He should know as much about God as humanly possible. The issue will be addressed, later in the chapter, VI, Who Is Man?

However as a lad, my knowledge about God's greatness and His Son's graciousness increased once I began to attend church regularly. One of the first tidbits of knowledge that I received at the church involved the Holy Spirit. I don't remember mother mentioning Him in her prayers (Yes, I said, Him, He is an alive personal Being). Maybe, like most people, mother did not know much about the operations of the Holy Spirit.

The Holy Spirit is the third Person of the Godhead, equal to the Son and the Father. They are three personalities, different in function, but one existence. Of the three, the Holy Spirit is the active participant operating in the world on behalf of the God, the Father and God, the Son.

In the book of Acts, He has often been described as speaking directly to men. He possesses intelligence, self-conscientiousness and self-determination in alignment with God's words.

Jesus said, "If I go not away, the Comforter will not come unto you; but if I depart, I will send Him unto you. Howbeit, when He, the Spirit of truth (Paraclete); is come, He will guide you into all truth" (John 16: 7; 13 KJV).

Note that the inclusion of the Holy Ghost (Spirit) into the equation completes the Doctrine of the Trinity. It was God the Father; that created all things. Paul spoke of the Father in Colossians, "giving thanks to the Father, who has qualified you to share in the inheritance of the saints in the kingdom of light. For He has rescued us from the dominion of darkness and brought us into the kingdom of the Son He loves, in whom we have redemption, the forgiveness of sins.

He is the image of the invisible God, the firstborn over all creation. **For by him all things were created:** things in heaven and on earth, visible and invisible, whether thrones or powers or rulers or authorities; **all things were created by him and for him.** He is before all things, and **in him all things hold together**" (or consist) (Colossians 1: 12-17 NIV).

The purpose of this chapter is to reveal as much about God as humanly possible. Since the question is, "Does God make me do what I do;" the first step in answering the question is to know God. By this I mean: To know who God is: what God has done, what God is doing and what God will do. Also just as important, it is to know what God will not do. So I ask; who is God? "God is **Spirit, infinite, eternal, and unchangeable in his being; wisdom, power, holiness, justice, goodness and truth**" [18]

GOD IS SPIRIT: Because there are other spiritual Beings, Jesus said, "God is "a" Spirit: and they that worship him must worship him in spirit and in truth" (John 4: 24). "It means that God is a non-material personal being, self-conscious and self-determining.

GOD IS INFINITE: The Psalm writer said, "Great is our Lord and of Great power: His understanding is infinite" (Psalm 147: 5). "It refers to the infinity of God, not an independent attribute. God is infinite in his being, without beginning or end. In other words, God is everywhere, all of the time.

The Omnipresence of God is vividly brought out through the Scriptures as in Psalm 139. God is not physically, relatively or measurably big. Some good theologians use the word immensity, but it conveys to some minds a false impression, as though God were partly here and partly there, like a giant or an amorphous mass or a fluid" [19]

But God's Omnipresence means that wherever we are, "even though we are like fleeing Jacob at Bethel (Gen. 28: 16), or on the run like Jonah (Jonah 1: 3) God is there. To understand this ideology better, let us say that God's omnipresence means, "Everything everywhere is immediately in his presence."

Finite creatures can act instantaneously, but in a limited area. But the Infinity of God means that every thing within his reach or sight is immediately in his presence, in the sense that distance is no problem. So in an absolutely perfect sense, every thing in the universe or in existence is immediately in the presence of God."[19]

He is wise: Wisdom denotes His omniscience (All knowing).

God's wisdom doesn't increase nor decrease. He eternally knows what he has known in the past and what he knows in the future. John says, "Whenever our hearts condemn us. For God is greater than our hearts, and he knows everything" (I John 3: 20 NIV).

He is Omnipotent: "All power has been given unto me" (Matthew 28: 18). The ability to do all that power can do: His controlling of all the power that is or can be.

God is Holy (Lev. 11: 44), **Just** (Isaiah 45: 21a) **and Good** (Psalm 100: 5): These words signify God's moral Attributes. Holy is purity. Justice is the administration of rewards and punishment. Goodness is his common grace toward all.

God is Truth: "It is impossible for God to lie" (Hebrews 6: 18 & Titus 1: 2). This attribute designates the basis of all logic and rationality. Logic and reason are attributes of God's character. Truth has nothing to do with power; it has to do with reality. Power can not change truth. For instance, how much power would it take to make 2+2=10?

God is Unchangeable: In Bible language, this points to the perfect self-consistency of God's character throughout all eternity. Nothing is contradictory in God." [19] Paul said, "Jesus Christ is the same yesterday, today and forever" (Hebrews 13: 8).

God is Love: "He that loveth not knoweth not God; for God is love (I John 4: 8) and He has love for his own. This is another important fact in the dissecting of the question; did God make me do it? Throughout the Scriptures those whom God has chosen to be "His own special people" (1Peter 2: 9), God has His eyes and ears on them. God calls these people in advance of the rest of humanity to be the "first-fruits" of billions whom He will ultimately include in His plan and bring into His family (James 1:18).

One such example of God's care even in the midst of martyrdom is found in the book of Acts, where Deacon Stephen proclaimed God's truth to a hostile crowd (Acts 6-7). Stephen's message incited a fatal reaction from the hearers and was stoned to death.

Continuation of the story revealed God supporting Stephen throughout the ordeal, from inspiring his words and actions to miraculously enlightening of his face as that of an angel. Even in death, God reassured Deacon Stephen with a dramatic vision of the Father and the Son in heaven."[18]

GOD IS CREATOR: "For by him was ALL THINGS created, that are in heaven and that are in earth, visible and invisible, whether they be thrones or dominion, or principalities or powers: ALL THINGS were created by him and for him." And he is before ALL THINGS and by him ALL THINGS consist" (Colossians 1: 16-17 KJV).

Genesis 1: 1, says, **"God created the heaven and the earth** and the earth was without form and void." From the first word written in this book, I have been trying to answer one of the great questions of history, where did evil come from?

The people that do not believe in God try to justify their unbelief by raising a similar question to the one above. They ask; if there is a God and he is good and loving, why did he create evil? Based upon this rationale, they conclude that either there is no God or that he is not good.

In response to the criticism by the Atheists and the like, some theologians have answered their attack on God by saying; the atheist's presupposition is flawed. In an attempt to get the Atheists off of their theological backs and defuse the agnostics from breathing down their hermeneutical throats, many have tried to take the easy way out of what they see as a theological dilemma.

They say to the Atheists, your premise is flawed because first of all, God did not create evil and therefore God is good. They say that God did not create evil, despite the texts that declare the opposite. The Scripture clearly indicates that God is the only Creator (Genesis 1: 1; Colossians 1: 16; Isaiah 40: 28). As such, there is but one conclusion to be drawn up and drank from the well of truth; **God created evil.**

Additionally, Isaiah 45 records the following words: "I form the light and create darkness: I make peace and **create evil: I the Lord do all these things**" (Isaiah 45: 7 KJV). The Proverbs of Solomon records, **"The Lord hath made all things for himself: yea, even the wicked for the day of evil"** (Proverbs 16: 4 KJV & RV).

Admittedly, it is highly debated and vigorously contested and difficult for some people to accept, nonetheless; it is the truth, the whole truth and nothing but the truth, so help me God. Think about it this way, if God for his own reasons created death, hell, and the grave, why is so difficult to believe that he created evil for his own reasons as well?

Let me add my declaration to the atheist's question on the goodness of God. God is good and in my humble opinion God's goodness is not in question. He created evil (Isaiah 45: 7; Proverbs 16: 4 & Col. 1: 16-17); but God is still good. He created death and have power over it (Genesis 2: 17 & Rev. 1: 18); but God is still good.

He created Hell and many people will end up there (Matthew 25: 41 & Luke 16: 19, etc.); but God is still good. In fact, unfortunately, there will more people in hell than in heaven. Jesus said so (Matthew 7: 13-14); but God is still good.

He created the grave and has power over it (Rev. 1: 18); but God is still good. Again I say to the Atheists and the like, the fact that God created evil, death, hell and the grave takes nothing away from His goodness. If I was in my pulpit preaching, I would say, and the church said, Amen.

So, what does the above information have to do with the question, "Does God make me do what I do?" **First of all,** the information about God was necessary to inform and assure us of who God is: That God has all of the power of Heaven, earth and Hell. In other words, God is Omnipotent, which means having all power in his hands (Matthew 28: 18). He has power over mankind, angels, but most importantly to our discussion, over the Devil. This is extremely good news for the human family.

Also, the love of God is important. While the Devil hates man, it's good to know that God loves man and will protect and provide for him "against the wiles of the Devil" (Eph. 6: 11 KJV). The great passage of John 3: 16 assure man of God's love. "God so loved the world that he gave his only begotten Son, that whosoever believeth in him, should not perish, but have everlasting life."

It's interesting to note that every time the Devil's (Satan) name is mentioned, it has to do with destruction (or the harm of some sort) of mankind. (REVIEW THE LIST ON PAGE 70, THE DEVILS' INTENTIONS TOWARD MANKIND.)

Yet whenever God's name is mentioned in Scripture, it had to do with blessings of the human family. At the hands of God, the episodes of pain and suffering occurred only when He (God) rendered justice in response to man's disobedience. Paul said, "Be not deceived, God is not mocked; whatsoever a man soweth, that shall he also reap" (Gal. 6: 7).

In other words, when it comes to wrong doing, man might get by, but he will not get away: What goes around; comes around: It's as sure as what goes up; must come down.

Second, the above information about God is twofold. While "whatsoever a man soweth, that shall he also reap" means that God will render justice, it also informs man that God will render grace and mercy. God is a God of purpose and protection.

Yet, the purpose and plan of the Devil is the exact opposite. Remember, Jesus said, "The Thief comest for to steal, kill and to destroy, but I am come that you might have life and have it more abundantly" (John 10: 10 KJV).

The real blessing of the verse centers around God and Christ' desire for man. It is good to know that God's will for man is to bless him, but it's even better to know that God is able to perform his will; over against the desires of the Devil.

With this knowledge, the confidence of man should skyrocket beyond the stars. The discovery that Satan has to attain God's permission to attack man is heart-warming and reassuring (Job 1-2). There's no where that this difference between God and the Devil more clearly seen than in the above passages of John 10: 10; and Job 1-2.

But it's just as clearly seen in Jesus' promise to Peter. Jesus said to him, "Simon, Simon, Satan desirest to have you that he may sift you as wheat. But I have am Prayed for thee, that thou faith fail not: and when thou art converted, strengthen thou brethren" (Luke 22: 31). In Genesis 3; John 8 and many other places in Scripture, it is also seen. There is no doubt about it; there are great differences between the Devil and God.

To the question, "Does God make me do what I do, there can be no doubt that God and God alone has the power to force man and every other creature (including the Devil) to do whatever God desires. Matthew 28: 18 affirms this fact: "And Jesus came and spake unto them, saying, all power is given unto me in heaven and the earth." So since God has the power to enforce his will, the question of necessity is, **"what is His Will or what does God want for man?"**

Any discussion that deals with the topic of what does God want for the human family has to begin with John 3: 16. John said, "For God so loved the world that he gave his one and only Son, that whoever believes in him shall not perish; but have eternal life. For God did not send his Son into the world to condemn the world; but to save the world through him" (John 3: 16-17 NIV).

Also, there are other's two cents of information that must be included into this nickel of knowledge. Peter said, "God is not slack concerning his promise, as some count slackness; but is longsuffering to usward, not willing that any should perish, but that all should come to repentance" (II Peter 3: 9 KJV).

Jesus said, "Go ye therefore and teach all nations, baptizing them in the name of the Father and of the Son and the Holy Ghost: Teaching them to observe all things whatsoever I have commanded you: and lo, I am with you always, even unto the end of the world. Amen" (Mathew 28: 19-20).

In Jesus' final departure as Savior, standing before the holy angels in the book of Acts, Jesus gave the church its marching orders. He said, "But ye shall receive power, after that the Holy Ghost is come upon you: and ye shall be witnesses unto me both in Jerusalem, and in all Judaea, and in Samaria, and unto the uttermost part of the earth" (Acts 1: 8 KJV).

Luke said, "The Son of man is come to seek and to save that which was lost" (Luke 19: 10 KJV). Matthew said, "The Son of man is come to save that which was lost" (Matt. 18: 11 KJV). Hopefully, the picture of the Devil is beginning to take shape and come together and his purpose, clearing up in the lens of man's vision and understanding.

"Ultimately the question of, what does God want for mankind is answered. God wants every man, woman, boy and girl to hear, understand and accept or reject Jesus Christ as their Savior and to be integrated into the local church, which renders accountability" [31]

In other words, God wants mankind to receive the gospel and have the opportunity for salvation in the exercise of their freewill. The following passages support man's choice to decide whether or not or to be saved: Mark 16: 15,16; Luke 24: 47; Titus 2: 11; 1 Timothy 2: 4,6; 2 Peter 3: 9; Hebrews 2: 9; John 3: 16; Acts 10: 34,35; Matthew 11: 28; Luke 2: 10; Genesis 2: 16,17; 3:1-7; 1 Corinthians 10: 13; Hebrews 4: 15; 11: 25; Joshua 24: 15; 1 Kings 18: 21; Psalm 119: 30.

"The "natural" man persists in determining his beliefs by human reasoning and intelligence instead of following the gospel. But the truth in religion can never be known this way, because man is not wise enough to figure it out.

So such people do not accept the things revealed by the Spirit. They consider such things foolish. This is what the Greeks were doing (I Cor. 1: 18- 23), and the Corinthians were being influenced by such thinking. The Free Will of man will be discussed more in chapter VII, entitled, why I really do what I do?

Yet, before the chapter closes, let me say one more word or two to the Atheists and any other non-believer. Man's Freewill is one of the main reasons that God created evil. The Genesis account of Creation revealed this fact.

Recorded in Genesis 2: 15; the Bible says, "And the Lord God took the man, and put him into the Garden of Eden to dress it and to keep it. And the Lord God commanded the man, saying, Of every tree of the garden thou mayest freely eat: But of the tree of the knowledge of good and evil, thou shalt not eat of it: for in the day that thou eatest thereof thou shalt surely die"(Genesis 2: 15-17 KJV).

First, the point is clear that evil was already created before man took of the Tree of the Knowledge of Good and Evil. Clearly, evil was already in existence. In Genesis one, make note of what the Bible records. It reads, "In the beginning, God created the heaven and the earth. And the earth was without form and void.

In other words, there was nothing here before God created the earth. There was nothing on the earth (It was without form and void) before God created the earth and place it here. The point is: God created evil before the creation of mankind and mankind had nothing to do with the existence of evil. Eve and Adam's sin brought the knowledge of evil into mankind's arena, but it existed somewhere, in the unknowns of God; as did death, pain and sorrow.

The second point in the creation story goes to the heart of the question of mankind's Free Will. Make note again that the Bible says, "And the Lord God commanded the man, saying, of every tree of the garden thou mayest freely eat: But of the tree of the knowledge of good and evil, thou shalt not eat of it: for in the day that thou eatest thereof thou shalt surely die" (Genesis 2: 17 KJV).

God gave mankind every tree to eat, with the exception of one. But stated, "for in the day that thou eatest there of, thou shalt surely die." The interpretative clarification is this, don't eat. But if you do eat; here are the consequences. God was informing the man of the choice (the Free Will that he had been given to choose) and the consequences that goes with the choice.

It is true that God did not have to give man the choice and could have forced man to obey him. But out of love and affection, God chose to extend man the privilege to fulfill his desires and choose his own way. This was an act of intelligence that God desired for mankind.

In like manner, obviously, mankind did not have to choose evil; man could have and should have chosen obedience: But he did not. Nonetheless, the "Fall of Mankind" was brought on by mankind, with the assistance of the Serpent (Devil). As has been dealt with, the Devil did not and can not make man do anything.

However, God could have made man do any and everything He wanted, but decided not to, out of love for human kind. The book has cited numerous Scriptures enumerating God's love for mankind (John 3: 16; John 10: 10; Luke 22: 31-32; Roman 5: 8, etc).

There can be no question about God's love for mankind. In fact, in the mind of most men, there is no question about it. It was God's love for mankind that gave the potential for evil as a consequence of man's Free Will. By giving him the Free Will to choose evil over good and the Devil over God is what led mankind into the valley of death and the consequences we see today.

Look at it this way: My wife (Frances Shaw Lomax) and I have been married thirty five years, with four children and two grand children. But when we first met, things did not seem to be headed toward the altar of matrimony.

When she decided to be my girlfriend, there was another fellow in the picture trying to date her as I was. Being a crafty and observant young man, I discovered the situation and the other man's involvement pretty quickly. Not knowing her intentions, immediately, I demanded that she choose between us.

To make a very long story as short as possible, she made the right choice and obviously chose me. But after she chose me over the other fellow (here's the point), our relationship grew closer than it had ever been before. If I had been the only good looking fellow on the earth and she had no other choice but me, I would not have known the joy of being chosen over a rival.

Consequently, our relationship would not have been as deep and loving or as reassuring and comforting as it has been. But the fact that she had another choice and out of love and deep attraction (excuse me, I meant deep affection), chose me over and above all of the others was sincerely satisfying.

From what we know about God through the word, the situation is similar between Him and humanity. God could have made man choose him, after all, He's God with all power in his hands. He didn't have to give mankind the gift of choice.

But he created evil and thus, gave us freewill that we might choose him out of deep love and attraction (to his goodness) in appreciation of his love and affection. Had there not been a choice or rival, the relationship could not have reached the highest heights of intimacy and affection.

The Omniscience of God demonstrated itself in the fact that God always knows what he is doing: the very definition of Omniscience. He gave us the gift of choice. We don't have to obey him. We have the choice to reject his love and accept the Devil's leadership. The choice is ours. Will you obey God and resist the Devil? Will you become or continue to be a living testimony against the Devil and for God, above and beyond the call of duty?

In the book of Job, the Devil raised these and some other significant challenges. He questioned God about mankind's sincerity in the declarations of love and piety. "Then Satan answered the LORD, and said, Doth Job fear God for nought" (Job 1: 9 KJV)? In short, the Devil accused mankind of pretense and hypocrisy. He said to God, mankind doesn't love you, but is only using you for their benefit.

More than six thousand years have passed, but the question is still as valid today as it was then. Reader, what kind of a relationship do you have with God? Did the Devil's accusation hit the target of your heart when it comes to your relationship with God? Do you love God?

Or do you love God for what He does and can do for you? What if He stops giving you blessings, would you stop adoring and worshipping Him? Has he done enough for you already that your love would last through out eternity?

Remember the Devil says, you would stop worshipping God if God stopped giving to you (Something to think about).

Finally, the answer to the question; "does God make us what we do" is a resounding no. The situation of Job adds more theological weight to the heavy stockpile of evidence already accumulated that God is in control. For the privilege of choice and free will, despite desperate times; Job honored God with love and devotion. Will you do the same?

In fact, Please note that it was after Job lost every material blessing imaginable, including the lives of all of his ten children, that he declared, "Naked came I out of my mother's womb and naked shall I return thither: the Lord gave and the Lord hath taken away; blessed be the name of the Lord. The Bible says, "In all this Job sinned not, nor charged God foolishly" (Job 1: 21-22 KJV).

Indeed, God is in control and has the power to force man to do whatever God desires, but back in the Garden of Eden, He chose and still chooses today to allow mankind the privilege of choice. What a mighty and loving God we serve. He does this in the hope that mankind will live up to its potential.

For the love of God and the privilege of Free Will, mankind needs to demonstrate appreciation rather than criticism. Stay tuned to station 1;1;1; for further information on the question: If the Devil didn't make me do it and God doesn't make me do it; who makes me do what I do? The answer is coming next in the following chapters, First, Who Is Man? Followed by, why I Really do What I Do?

But before moving on to the next chapter, write down at least three tidbits of information learned from the above chapter.

1._____

2._____

3._____

CHAPTER VII
WHO IS MAN?

"What is man, that thou art mindful of him? and the son of man, that thou visitest him? For thou hast made him a little lower than the angels, and hast crowned him with glory and honour. Thou madest him to have dominion over the works of thy hands; thou hast put all things under his feet" (Psalm 8: 4-6).

"But one in a certain place testified, saying, What is man, that thou art mindful of him? or the son of man, that thou visitest him? Thou madest him a little lower than the angels; thou crownedst him with glory and honour, and didst set him over the works of thy hands: Thou hast put all things in subjection under his feet. For in that he put all in subjection under him, he left nothing that is not put under him. But now we see not yet all things put under him.

But we see Jesus, who was made a little lower than the angels for the suffering of death, crowned with glory and honour; that he by the grace of God should taste death for every man. For it became him, for whom are all things, and by whom are all things, in bringing many sons unto glory, to make the captain of their salvation perfect through sufferings" (Hebrews 2: 6-10 KJV).

The subject of mankind is one that humans know much about. But when placed under the microscopic lens of examination, it could be discovered that humans don't know as much as they think. Yet, conceding that; man does know more about mankind than about the Devil or God. The reason for this knowledge is obvious; humans lives with mankind: Humans see and interacts with them on a daily basis.

Human's knowledge of mankind includes many facts. One such fact is man's capability to lie; everyday, he sees, hears and reads about his/her lies in the news. Through the same avenues, mankind knows that humans are capable of murder, fornication, adultery, drunkenness, rape and child molestation.

Additionally, human beings are abusive in marriage: with husbands beating wives and sometimes wives doing the same to the husband. As a result, the children are victimized as well. The list of atrocities that human beings are capable of is long and in exhaustive.

Several times during the book, the question has been raised, what happened to mankind? In scripture, it is clear that the manner in which mankind is living now is not how God intended man to live. First, it must be noted that God created man in his image and likeness. Second, God created man to bless him and have him represent (or re-present) God throughout the earth.

In the book of Genesis, Moses wrote the following, "Then God said, "Let us make man in our image, in our likeness, and let them rule over the fish of the sea and the birds of the air, over the livestock, over all the earth, and over all the creatures that move along the ground.

So God created man in his own image, in the image of God he created him; male and female he created them. "God blessed them and said to them, "Be fruitful and increase in number; fill the earth and subdue it. Rule over the fish of the sea and the birds of the air and over every living creature that moves on the ground" (Genesis 1: 28 NIV). This was the intended action of the man God created.

Also set under the microscopic lens of examination is the question; what does it mean to be created in the image of God? The question has been raised countless times over the years. "Probably the greatest answer is found in looking at the difference in mankind verses all of the other creatures of creation.

As God's highest creation, a major difference is man's ability to exercise moral choice. Since God is all-knowing (Review previous chapter); He can envision all of the possible choices. Since He is all-wise, He can discern, exactly, which choices are perfect and which are not worth choosing.

Since He is all-powerful, He can choose that perfectly wise choice that is His will and exclude all others for eternity. **Man is similarly** allowed to think of a variety of choices, choose an action, and consider the wisdom of his choice.

Animals only react to environment. Angels exercised choice only once and are eternally sealed into that choice; good angels cannot choose not to worship and obey; evil angels cannot be saved and cannot choose to worship and obey. Choice is an important God like ability in line with the Image of God.

We read in Colossians 1:15 where Christ is "the image of the invisible God." The Greek word here is *"icon"* (image of the invisible God) which is the same word used in the Septuagint for Genesis 1:27. (The Septuagint is the Greek translation of the Hebrew Bible.)

Since the image of God in man is so debated and at times can seem so philosophically obscure, if we want to understand what it means to be created in the image and likeness of God, we must ultimately look to Jesus who is "the radiance of God's glory" as well as the "exact representation of His nature" (Heb 1:3). [22]

As stated earlier, Jesus (the second Adam) fulfilled all that the first Adam failed. In Jesus we see God's perfect image and likeness in human form. John said, "And the Word became flesh and dwelt among us and we beheld his glory, the glory as the only begotten of the father full of grace and truth" (John 1: 14 KJV).

On the image of God, Pope Benedict XVI, put it this way. "The basic material is earth; from this the human being comes into existence after God has breathed his breath into the nostrils of the body that was formed from it. The divine reality enters in here.

The first creation account, which we considered in our previous meditations, says the same thing by way of another and more deeply reflective image. It says that the human being is created in God's image and likeness (Gen 1:26-27).

In the human being, heaven and earth touch one another. In the human being, God enters into his creation; the human being is directly related to God. The human being is called by him. God's words in the Old Testament are valid for every individual human being: I call you by name and you are mine.

Each human being is known by God and loved by him. Each is willed by God, and each is God's image. Precisely in this consists the deeper and greater unity of humankind -- that each of us, each individual human being, realizes the *one* project of God and has his or her origin in the same creative idea of God. Hence the Bible says that whoever violates a human being violates God's property" (Gen 9:5). [23]

If man was created in the image and likeness of God and he was; it is important to know that man was created with God in him. Therefore man has knowledge, wisdom and the power of choice, which the lower animals do not possess. Both Psalm 8 and Hebrews 2 enlightened us of man's preeminent stature in the Creation story.

A modern reading of the main text of the chapter and exegesis adds more in sight to the question of who is man. It reads, **"But there is a place where someone has testified: "What is man that you are** mindful of him, the son of man that you care for him? You made him a little lower than the angels; you crowned him with glory and honor and put everything under his feet."

In putting everything under him, God left nothing that is not subject to him. Yet at present we do not see everything subject to him (because of sin). But we see Jesus, who was made a little lower than the angels, now crowned with glory and honor because he suffered death, so that by the grace of God he might taste death for everyone.

In bringing many sons to glory, it was fitting that God, for whom and through whom everything exists, should make the author of their salvation perfect through suffering. Both the one who makes men holy and those who are made holy are of the same family. So Jesus is not ashamed to call them brothers.

He says, "I will declare your name to my brothers; in the presence of the congregation I will sing your praises." And again, "I will put my trust in him." And again he says, "Here am I, and the children God has given me." Since the children have flesh and blood, he too shared in their humanity so that by his death he might destroy him who holds the power of death--that is, the devil--" (Hebrews 2: 6-10 NIV).

In these verses, not only do we see man's status in God, but also Jesus.' Man was created a little lower than the angels enclosed with flesh and blood, yet he sinned. Therefore, Jesus was born into flesh and blood to share man's humanity and by his death and resurrection as a sinless human being; both justified man's sin and at the same time destroyed the power of the Devil who holds the reigns on death.

Therefore, the will of God for each individual human being can only be obtained through a relationship with Him and the proper representation of Him throughout the earth. For after all, man was created by God to relate to God, be blessed by God and represent (Re-present) God in the earth.

"His body was created pure and good (Gen. 1:31); there was nothing inherently evil or sinful about it. [26] In light of man's creation and purpose in contrast to the undeniable evidence of mankind's degenerate state today, the question arises, again, what happened to mankind?

Why the husband with a good wife and family risks it all for a one night stand? Why the wife with a good hard working husband and great children risks it all in an affair on the job? Why are there so many boyfriends killing their girlfriends and ending up dead themselves or spending the rest of their lives in prison?

Why are there so many old men and women enticing young boys and girls to satisfy their perverse desires? Even in the scholastic arena, why are there so many experienced adult female teachers romantically involved with innocent children with no experience?

As highlighted in the book, earlier, why are there so many mass murders taking place and the total disregard for human life? The attempt to list all of the whys of human tragedy; is, in and of itself, a human tragedy. What happened to the creation that God looked at and said, "Behold, it was very good" (Genesis 1: 31)?

Here's the Biblical explanation. "After the "Fall," the body that God created (and said, was very good) became different. It changed to what the Scripture now refers to as "flesh, which in the Scriptures has at least three meanings: the flesh of our physical body (John 6:55); the fallen, corrupted body contaminated by sin (Rom. 7:18); and the fallen man (Rom. 3:20).

It needs noting that God did not create fallen flesh; He created a body of flesh, blood, and bones. When man fell (by the sin of Adam and Eve), sin, the evil nature of Satan, came into man's body, transmuting it into "the flesh." This flesh is called "the flesh of sin" (Rom. 8: 3, Gk.)

and the fallen body is called "the body of sin" (Rom. 6: 6) and "the body of this death" (Rom. 7:24).

Because the God-created body has been corrupted and ruined by sin and transmuted into the flesh, all kinds of lusts are now members of our body" (Gal. 5:24; Col. 3:5).[26] It was through sin that man became "the children of the Devil" (I John 3: 10 KJV). It was through Christ that man became "the children of God."

Make note that man was created with the potential for greatness; but also the possibility for sin and shame. In this a true demonstration of God's love was seen. God loved mankind enough to run the risk of losing him. As has been said before, "Love lets go and if it returns, it was true love and meant to be." Love can not be bought or imprisoned. Love must be free to spread its wings, if it is love.

God has repeatedly shone love for man and one would think that Man's love for God would have been reciprocated beyond penetration by the Devil or any other creature. It should have been as solid as a rock. However, history reports a different finding. In the courtroom of Justice, at the trial of man, history could be called as a witness to testify that man rejected the love of God and sinned against him without cause.

When given the choice to reciprocate God's love, man turned against him and sided with his archenemy. He disobeyed God, listened to the Devil and yielded to the desires of the flesh. To which he has repeatedly yielded ever since.

It was the "Fall" that corrupted man's body, mind and spirit and brought other serious consequences into the human arena. Such as the eventual death of man's body and his sin sick nature. After the "Fall" man was a different creature. In his book, entitled, <u>Disturbed about Man,</u> Dr. Benjamin Mayes addressed man's dilemma.

He said: "I'm not disturbed about God; I'm not disturbed about the Devil. I am disturbed about man. I am uneasy about man. I am uneasy about man because there is no guarantee, no infallible proof that he is going to make it on the earth, no guarantee that he is going to pull through.

I am uneasy about man because God in creating man; faced the awful dilemma of making a free personality with potentialities for good and evil, or making him a machine without power of choice and without personality. So in making man free to choose, he had to make him free to choose right or wrong, truth or falsehood, peace or war, the high road or the low road.

This point of view is supported by the eminent theologian Paul Tillich. He said in Volume II of his Systematic Theology: **"It is the image of God in man which gives the possibility of "The Fall" (of Adam and Eve). Only he who is the image of God has the power of separating himself from God. His greatness and his weakness are identical.**

Even God could not remove the one without removing the other. And if man had not received this possibility, he would have been a thing among things, unable to serve the divine glory, either in salvation or in condemnation."[24]

"For in the former, God as Creator demanded perfect obedience from innocent man with the promise of life and eternal happiness; but in the latter, God as Father promises salvation in Christ to the fallen man under the condition of faith.

The former rested upon the work of man, the latter upon the grace of God alone: The former upon a just Creator; the latter upon a merciful Redeemer. The former was made with innocent man without a mediator; the latter was made with fallen man by the intervention of a mediator.

The covenant of nature is that which God the Creator made with innocent man as his creature, concerning the giving of eternal happiness and life under nature:" The condition of perfect and personal obedience. It is called "natural," not from natural obligation (which God does not have towards man), but because it is founded on the nature of man (as it was at first created by God) and on his integrity of powers.

It is also called "legal" because man's condition was the observation of the law of nature, engraved within him; and of "works" because it depended upon works or proper obedience.[20]

After the fall: The greatest and most obvious change of consequence was death. The death was twofold. (A). It was partly physical or the separation of the soul from the body. With the choice to disobey God came the seeds of death (that had been implanted within man) began to develop themselves the moment that access to the tree of life was denied him. Man from that moment was a dying creature.

But the death was also and more chiefly (B), spiritual death or the separation of the soul from God. In this is included, negatively, the loss of man's moral likeness to God or that the underlying tendency of his whole nature toward God, which constituted his original righteousness was corrupted. In other words, spiritual death blinded man's intellect; corrupted his affections and enslaved his will.

Seeking to become a god, man became a slave. Seeking independence, he ceased to be the master of himself. In the decision to no longer make God the end of his life, he chose self instead. While he retained the power of self-determination in subordinate things, he lost the freedom that consisted in the power of choosing God as his ultimate aim and became fettered by a fundamental inclination of his will toward evil." [26]

By choosing the Devil's course of action in the Garden of Eden, man chose to give himself over to him, lock, stock and barrel. By his decision, he not only changed his makeup, he also changed the makeup of the Garden of Eden.

It was created a place without sin, shame and sorrow. It was created a place of paradise where God would have fellowship from loving and obedient creatures: A place that God would literally come down in the cool of the day and converse and fellowship with mankind.

Yet man's failure to reverence, honor God's rules of operation and exercise the free will God gave; changed the environment. It was changed so drastically, that God had no choice; but banishment of him from the garden.

On the positive side, death for the believer is the way to reunite with God and spend eternity in praise to Him for his sacrifice. For God so loved us in spite of our disobedience and bad choices, he prepared a place for us in the heavens. Because of Jesus, the power to choose our final destination has been restored to us.

Look at the writer of Hebrews. He said, **"But we see Jesus, who was made a little lower than the angels, now crowned with glory and honor because he suffered death, so that by the grace of God he might taste death for everyone.**

In bringing many sons to glory, it was fitting that God, for whom and through whom everything exists, should make the author of their salvation perfect through suffering. Both the one who makes men holy and those who are made holy are of the same family. So Jesus is not ashamed to call them brothers" (Hebrews 2: 9-11 NIV).

Again we thank God for the Free Will of choice. In the last chapter, God's gift of Free Will to man was briefly brought up. But, in this chapter, it will be further defined. Again, when we speak of man's Free Will, primarily we are speaking of the **"God given ability to make choices without any prior prejudice, inclination, or disposition," and specifically that these "free will" choices are not ultimately predestined by God.** [27]

If mankind would just make up its mind to follow God, the world would be a much better place to live. The following are some of the situations that Man's Free Will were exercised. There has already been much discussion of Adam and Eve's choice.

So let us examine a pareticular example in Joshua's day. The prophet Joshua said to the Children of Israel, "But if serving the Lord seems undesirable to you, then choose for yourselves this day, whom you will serve; whether the gods your forefathers served beyond the River, or the gods of the Amorites, in whose land you are living. But as for me and my household, we will serve the LORD.

Then the people answered, "Far be it from us to forsake the LORD to serve other gods! It was the LORD our God himself who brought us and our fathers up out of Egypt, from that land of slavery, and performed those great signs before our eyes.

He protected us on our entire journey and among all the nations through which we traveled. And the LORD drove out before us all the nations, including the Amorites, who lived in the land. We too will serve the LORD, because he is our God.

Joshua said to the people, you are not able to serve the LORD. He is a holy God; he is a jealous God. He will not forgive your rebellion and your sins. If you forsake the LORD and serve foreign gods, he will turn and bring disaster on you and make an end of you, after he has been good to you." But the people said to Joshua, "No! We will serve the LORD" (Joshua 24: 15: -21 NIV). They said that they would serve the Lord, but did not.

Another example of the gift of Free will to man is reflected in II Chron. 7: 14. God says, "If my people which are called by my name shall humble themselves and pray, seek my face, turn from their wicked ways: Then will I hear from heaven and forgive their sins and heal the land."

What about in the destruction recorded in book of Judges? The Bible says, "When new gods were chosen, then war was in the gates" (Judges 5: 8 NRSV). Who can forget the great debate of history over mankind's all time worse use of Free Will?

Which one of them was the worst, the bad choice of Adam and Eve or the people's terrible choice of Barabbas over Jesus? Remember, "the governor again said to them, "Which of the two do you want me to release for you?" And they said, "Barabbas" (Matt. 27: 21 NRSV).

COMMERCIAL BREAK:

Out of a strong desire to help the human family, pleased allow me the privilege to share with you the source of my strength in times of burden; and the times that I feel that the weight of the world is on my shoulders. Moses' strength in times of burden was his rod. Sampson's source of strength was his hair. My strength is in the above account of Jesus and Barabbas.

The Scripture informs us that the Jewish leaders demanded the death of Jesus. Governor Pontius Pilate did not find any fault in the man. Pilate's wife informed him of the dream she had concerning Jesus. She asked him not to have anything to do with the death of this just man. Pilate thought seriously about her words and decided to abide by them.

He knew of an old Jewish custom that at the Passover (John 18: 39), out of mercy, he could release a prisoner of the people's choice. He informed Jesus of his decision to release a prisoner unto the people of their choice.

I know that this decision of Pilate was received well by Jesus. In fact, I sensed Jesus' excitement of the opportunity for the people to decide his fate.

After all, it would take the remainder of the book to recount all of the people that Jesus, either healed or helped in some major manner: People that would be present or should have been there for him in his hour of need. People like blind Bartimaeus, the blind man of John nine; Lazarus, Jairus's daughter, the woman with the issue of blood, Mary Magdalene and so many others.

To prove the point Biblically, Matthew says, "And many women were there beholding afar off, which followed Jesus from Galilee, ministering unto him: Among which was Mary Magdalene, and Mary the mother of James and Joses, and the mother of Zebedee's children. When the even was come, there came a rich man of Arimathaea, named Joseph, who also himself was Jesus' disciple" (Matt. 27: 55-57 KJV). So Jesus had a right to feel safe and secure.

Moreover, at the discovery of the person that he would be standing beside for the choice, had to heighten his excitement. Barabbas was a known thief and murderer. Surely, they would not choose such a man over Jesus, he must have thought. So, the decision of the people was a no brainer for Jesus.

Yet, when Pilate put forth the question, "Which of the two do you want me to release for you?" And they said, "Barabbas" (Matt. 27: 21 NIV), Jesus had the shock of his life.

The decision of the people had to let the wind out of His sails. The disappointment in the people's choice could not be placed into words, except to say that it had to be devastating. Remember Jesus was both human and God.

However, as devastating as that decision was, the next one was even more so. "Pilate said to them, "Then what should I do with Jesus who is called the Messiah?" All of them said, "Let him be crucified!" Then he asked, "Why, what evil has he done?" But they shouted all the more, "Let him be crucified" (Matt. 27: 22-23 NRSV)!

Luke says, "Pilate' desire was to just chastise Jesus and let him go" (Luke 23: 16). So, crucifixion was not the only choice that the people had. They could have chosen to chastise him as Pilate desired. They could have imprisoned him and obviously, they could have released him. But to scream crucify him, crucify him, was then and now, unconscionable and inexplicable.

Therefore when unconscionable and inexplicable events come my way as I perform ministry, I think about what was done to Christ, Jesus. His suffering makes a great difference in my mental capacity to continue when dealing with the evils of the world.

END OF THE COMMERCIAL BREAK!

Down through the Centuries, the debate of Man's Free Will has been hot and heavy. One of the arguments presented by the founding father's of theology at the various councils (The Council of Nicea, etc) involved the question; would Mankind have been better off today, physically and spiritually, if God had not given him the gift of Free Will?

There are some that say yes. They emphasize the point that if God had not given mankind the gift of Free Will, there would have been a need for evil. No evil; No choice of evil. No choice of evil; No pain, sorrow, death, hell or the grave into mankind's arena of life.

However, the people that say, mankind would have been better off without Free Will, forget the purpose of the creation of mankind. **(1)** God created mankind for God to have someone to relate to: A being of high intellect and moral integrity like God, Himself.

God desired such beings to be around him like himself. Thereby, man was not created to be a robot, functioning without attributes of love, affection, reasoning, etc. God wanted a being that in the cool of the day; He could come down and communicate with on a high level closer to that of God than the lower animals.

John tells us that God is love (I John 4: 8) and love gives. In fact, love is fulfilling only while giving. So God is both fulfilling and happy when He is giving.

(2) Thus, also, God created man for the purpose of having someone to bless and to give too. But in giving; God wanted someone to give to; that could and would not only appreciate the blessing; but the Blessor and in return bless others.

(3) God created mankind to replenish the earth and represent (or re-present) Him in the earth. A robot could not fulfill God's purpose for the creation: **Only Mankind.**

The expression of honor and appreciation is heard in the voice of the Psalmist for mankind's creation. He said, **"You made him (man) a little lower than the heavenly beings and crowned him with glory and honor. You made him ruler over the works of your hands; you put everything under his feet: all flocks and herds, and the beasts of the field, the birds of the air, and the fish of the sea, all that swim the paths of the seas. O Lord, our Lord, how majestic is your name in all the earth! (Psalm 8: 5-9 NIV).**

As reflected above, God deserves praise for the creative order of things. It only makes that when praises go up; blessings come down. Think about it, who doesn't like flattery? Stay tuned to the remaining question, **"Why do I really do what I do?"**

But before moving on to the next chapter, write down at least three tidbits of information learned from the above chapter.

1._____

2._____

3._____

CHAPTER VIII
WHY I REALLY DO WHAT I DO?

"I do not understand what I do. For what I want to do I do not do, but what I hate I do. And if I do what I do not want to do, I agree that the law is good. As it is, it is no longer I myself who do it, but it is sin living in me. I know that nothing good lives in me, that is, in my sinful nature. For I have the desire to do what is good; but I cannot carry it out.

For what I do is not the good I want to do; no, the evil I do not want to do--this I keep on doing. Now if I do what I do not want to do, it is no longer I who do it, but it is sin living in me that does it. So I find this law at work: When I want to do good, evil is right there with me. For in my inner being I delight in God's law; but I see another law at work in the members of my body, waging war against the law of my mind and making me a prisoner of the law of sin at work within my members.

What a wretched man I am! Who will rescue me from this body of death? Thanks be to God--through Jesus Christ our Lord! So then, I myself in my mind am a slave to God's law, but in the sinful nature a slave to the law of sin" (Romans 7: 15-25 NIV).

"I write to you, children, because you know the Father. I write to you, fathers, because you know him who is from the beginning. I

write to you, young people, because you are strong and the word of God abides in you, and you have overcome the evil one. Do not love the world or the things in the world.

The love of the Father is not in those who love the world; for all that is in the world--the desire of the flesh, the desire of the eyes, the pride in riches--comes not from the Father but from the world. And the world and its desire are passing away, but those who do the will of God live forever" (I JOHN 2: 14-17 NRSV).

Through the preponderance of Scripture, the book has already given evidence that the Devil (Satan, the evil one) speaks to man attempting to entice him into disobedience of God and have him on the pathway to destruction. Briefly remember that in the Garden of Eden, he convinced Eve and Adam to disobey God (Genesis 3: 1 KJV) and we know the tragic result.

The Bible says, Satan stood up against Israel and provoked King David to number Israel. King David was on the verge of war with the Philistines and was afraid of their great number. Under the influence of Satan, he ordered Joab to go and number Israel (I Chron. 21: 1-2 KJV). David wanted to see how the numbers would line up, instead of trusting God. Obviously, "God was not pleased with the thing," as verse number seven indicates, "therefore, God smote Israel."

The command from God is always the same, yesterday, today and forevermore, "Trust in the LORD with all thine heart; and lean not unto thine own understanding. In all thy ways acknowledge him, and he shall direct thy paths. Be not wise in thine own eyes: fear the LORD, and depart from evil. It shall be health to thy navel and marrow to thy bones" (Proverb 3: 5-8 KJV).

Out in the wilderness of Jordan, Satan in conversation with Jesus tried to get Him to disobey God" (Matt. 4: 1-11). The reason was obvious, get Jesus to obey Satan and disobey God: No sinless Jesus, No sinless Savior. No sinless Savior, No Salvation. End of story.

Within the passage of Luke 22: 3, Satan entered into Judas and inspired him to go out and betray Jesus. However, it needs stating that Satan can only enter into a willing vessel and with the permission of God. This is evidenced in God's conversation with Satan where He allows him only to go so far in the attack on Job (Job 1-2).

James verifies the fact too that man can resist the Devil if he wants. He said, "Submit yourselves therefore to God. Resist the Devil and he will flee from you. Draw nigh to God and he will draw nigh to you." (James 4: 7-8 KJV).

Matthew detailed Peter's attempt to rebuke Jesus for Jesus' revelation to the disciples. He informed them of his planned course of action for the next few days, which included his death, burial and resurrection. Matthew 16: 23 says, "But He (Jesus) turned, and said unto Peter, Get thee behind me, Satan: thou art an offence unto me: for thou savourest not the things that be of God, but those that be of men" (KJV).

Under the inspiration of Satan, Peter tried to convince Jesus to change his course of action. But Jesus recognized Satan's words, even though, it was Peter's voice.

Throughout the book, I have been trying impart several necessary nuggets of truth. One of them is as follows: the first step of necessity in defeating Satan in the every day walk of life is to recognize his words, language and speech. In order to accomplish the recognition of his words, language and speech, no matter whose voice is heard or how familiar, **the acknowledgement of Satan's existence is mandatory.**

Unfortunately, this is not nearly as easy as it sounds. It is a major hurdle. In the world, there are millions of people that do not acknowledge or believe in the existence of the Devil. The numbers have already been submitted on page five. Borrowing a line from the late James Brown, "say it loud," and I add the words, **the Devil is real: the Devil is real.**

As already said, there aren't as many people that don't believe in God as don't believe in the Devil. It seems as though, if you believe in the existence of one of them, you should more likely to believe in the existence of the other. If you do not believe in the existence of one of them, you are more likely not to believe in the existence of the other.

Inexplicable, however, there is some deviation from these facts as pointed out earlier. As stated, 78% of Americans believe in Heaven and God while only about 55% or so believe in the existence of Hell and the Devil.

Yet, once again, I must borrow a line for the late James Brown, "say it loud," and I add the words, **God is real: God is real.** The Psalmist said, "Only the fool hath said in his heart, there is no God. They are corrupt, and their ways are vile; there is none that does good.

God looks down from heaven on the sons of men to see if there are any who understand, any who seek God. Everyone has turned away, they have together become corrupt; there is no one who does good; not even one.

Will the evildoers never learn-- those who devour my people as men eat bread and who do not call on God? There they were, overwhelmed with dread, where there was nothing to dread. God scattered the bones of those who attacked you; you put them to shame, for God despised them" **(Psalm 14: 1; & 53: 1-5 NIV).**

In order to defeat the Devil and receive the blessings of the Lord, we must believe that they both exist. Yet, we must not only believe in their existence, we must acknowledge it openly and with conviction.

As far as the Devil is concerned, we will never defeat him without acknowledging his existence. It is even unconscionable to imagine anyone going into battle without any acknowledgement of the enemy. In fact, if there is no acknowledgement of the enemy's existence, there would be no need for battle. It's like arguing, "It's hard to argue by yourself."

The necessity of acknowledging the enemy has Biblical support. Recorded in the 14th chapter of the book of Numbers, Moses sent out the twelve spies to determine the enemy, his strengths and weaknesses, etc.

The same must be done in the war against the Devil. The first step is to acknowledge his existence. To which the numbers conclude that most Americans have not done. Therefore, the surprise or the amazement of the Devil having his way in the lives of most human beings is not surprising at all.

However, the time for man's acknowledgement of his existence is long over due. Sooner or later, for man's own benefit, he must realize that every minute of every day and in every way possible; Satan attempts to influence us against God.

The conflicts that you and I face are not about humanity. They have little to do with flesh and blood. The conflicts are spiritual and have their origin in God and the Devil. I really don't like being redundant, but Paul informed us of the battle and the combatants.

He said, "For our struggle is not against enemies of blood and flesh, but against the rulers, against the atrocities, against the cosmic powers of this present darkness, against the spiritual forces of evil in the heavenly places" (Eph. 6: 11 NIV). To the question: How do we win the war?

Paul said, "Therefore take up the whole armor of God, so that you may be able to withstand on that evil day, and having done everything, to stand firm.

Stand therefore, and fasten the belt of truth around your waist, and put on the breastplate of righteousness. As shoes for your feet put on whatever will make you ready to proclaim the gospel of peace.

With all of these, take the shield of faith, with which you will be able to quench all the flaming arrows of the evil one. Take the helmet of salvation, and the sword of the Spirit, which is the word of God. Pray in the Spirit at all times in every prayer and supplication. To that end keep alert and always persevere in supplication for all the saints" (Eph. 6: 12-18 NRSV).

After the acknowledgement of the Devil's existence, we need to learn how to distinguish his voice, language and speech. His language is always negative, demeaning and destructive. Consider I Chronicles 21: 1; Job 1-2; Matthew 16: 23 and Luke 22: 3. If the Devil ever inspires a positive word, it is short lived. Just keep your eyes and ears open for a little while and you will discover that he's only using the positive to set up the negative.

Therefore, it is imperative to know God's word because Satan knows it. Remember Satan was an arch angel and in Matthew 4, he tried to change it to fool Jesus (Matthew 4: 6). If man can not distinguish between the two, it will lead to certain destruction.

Example: remember how he changed God's words and flattered Eve in the garden. Those flattering words were used to deceive man for the set up of history. Please note: Satan's flattery worked on Eve. Remember, He told her that she and Adam would not die, if they ate from the forbidden tree (Gen. 3: 4): indicating that they would continue to live forever.

They listened to him and died. If you don't believe they died, look up their names in the telephone directory, you will not find them listed. They both died and so did their children and their children's children.

The Serpent told them that they would "be as gods" (Gen. 3: 5), if they listened to him. They listened to him and did not become as gods. In fact, listening to the flattering words of the Devil caused them not only to be ran out of the paradise of God; but also, almost to be ran out of existence.

However, the tactics of the Devil that worked on Adam and Eve had no chance to work on Jesus. As you know, he tried three times to fool Jesus in the wilderness, only to end up being the fool (Matt. 4: 1-11).

As the young people would say; he tried to play Jesus, only to end up being played. In other words, "The player got played." Jesus exhorts us to be aware of his tactics and "not be ignorant of his devices" (II Cor. 2: 11). Remember Jesus Knows God's words.

I will not insult your intelligence by restating here all of the many Scriptures already presented in the earlier chapters indicating the Devil's plans for you and me. Neither will I insult your intelligence by restating the many Scriptures already presented in the earlier chapters, indicating God's purpose and plans for the human family.

Yet, I will state, declare and proclaim that the plan of God and the plan of the Devil for mankind are as far apart as the East is from the West and the North is from the South.

Whereas Satan wants to kill, steal and destroy us, God, the Father, the Son and the Holy Ghost wants us to live and live more abundantly (John 10: 10). Whereas Satan wants to sift us as wheat (break us down into nonexistence), Jesus is praying for us to be converted and saved (Luke 22: 31).

Whereas Satan wants us to obey him and disobey God and do anything to make ends meet and satisfy our physical desires, God wants us to live by every word that proceedeth out of the mouth of God (Matt. 4: 4).

Whereas Satan wants us to show off and show out and mistreat the Holy things of God, Jesus says, thou shalt not tempt the Lord thy God (Matt. 4: 7).

Whereas Satan wants us to worship the material things of the world, cars, houses, gold, power and position, etc; Jesus wants us to have these things, but says, "But seek first his kingdom and his righteousness, and all these things will be given to you as well" (Matt. 6: 33 NIV).

He also says, "worship the Lord thy God and him only shalt thou serve" (Matt. 4: 10 KJV). So now we come to the heart of the book, the moral of the message and the critical question of our generation, **"Why do I really do what I do?"**

On one hand, the Devil stands and whispers one thing in our ears. On the other hand, God stands and whispers something else in the other. On one hands, the Devil tells us to get drunk, relax and have a little fun.

On the other hand, God says, "Be sober, be vigilant (be watchful and alert); because your adversary, the Devil as a roaring lion, walketh about, seeking whom he may devour" (I Peter 5: 8 NEB).

God tells us, "Do not get drunk with wine, for that is debauchery; but be filled with the Spirit, as you sing psalms and hymns and spiritual songs among yourselves, singing and making melody to the Lord in your hearts" (Ephesians 5: 18- 19 RSV). "What do I do?"

On one hand, the Devil tells us to steal, kill and destroy (John 10: 10). On the other hand, God tells us to give, heal, and build. "It is more blessed to give than to receive" (Acts 20: 35 KJV). "What do I do?"

On one hand, the Devil tells us to have sexual relations outside of marriage. On the other hand, God tells us, "Marriage should be honored by all, and the marriage bed kept pure, for God will judge the adulterer and all the sexually immoral" (Hebrews 13: 4 NIV). "What do I do?"

On one hand, the Devil tells us to put drugs in our bodies, by mouth, arm or leg, etc. On the other hand, God asked us, "Do you not know that your body is a temple of the Holy Spirit, who is in you, whom you have received from God? You are not your own; you were bought at a price.

Therefore honor God with your body" (I Cor. 6: 19-20 NIV). Also the Bible tells us to "Present your bodies a living sacrifice, holy, acceptable unto God, which is your reasonable service" (Romans 12: 1b KJV). "What do I do?"

On one hand the Devil tells us to break our curfews and stay out late at night. On the other hand, God tells all of the "Children, to obey your parents in the Lord, for this is right."Honor your father and mother"-- which is the first commandment with a promise-- "that it may go well with you and that you may enjoy long life on the earth" (Eph. 6: 1-3 NIV).

The reason Satan tells us to disobey our parents, he knows that it will hurt us and shorten our life spans. The question remains, "What Do I do?" The answers seem obvious to me, but the choice is yours.

Make note that it is not what I say, it's what I do. So every day, faced with these dilemmas and predicaments of choice, what do I do? The Devil on one hand and God on the other, "what do I do?" Good on one hand, evil on the other, "what do I do?" Obedience on one hand, sin on the other, "what do I do?'

What do I do when many around me, in the neighborhood, school, and on the television; When the whole world seems to be stealing, killing, doing drugs, getting drunk, fornicating, breaking curfews and sinning in general? What do I do?

The first suggestion is to take some time and meditate on the situation in light of the word of God. In the Bible, there is an answer to every question. The Psalmist said, "Blessed is the man who does not walk in the counsel of the wicked or stand in the way of sinners or sit in the seat of mockers.

But his delight is in the law of the LORD, and on his law he **meditates** day and night. He is like a tree planted by streams of water, which yields its fruit in season and whose leaf does not wither. Whatever he does prospers" Psalm 1: 1-3 NIV).

On the other hand, the Psalmist declared that its "Not so with the wicked! They are like chaff that the wind blows away. Therefore the wicked will not stand in the judgment, nor sinners in the assembly of the righteous. For the LORD watches over the way of the righteous, but the way of the wicked will perish" (Psalm 1: 4-6 NIV).

It's been proven Biblically that the Devil can only influence us. He can not make us to anything. Also, it's been proven Biblically that God can force us to do his will, but He will not force us. He will only instruct and remind us of his will, the choice is ours to make. Remember "Free Will" is a gift from God. We did nothing to earn it. God gave it to mankind purely out of love and hope for our enrichment.

But what exactly is Free Will? "Probably the most common definition of free will is the **"God given ability to make choices without any prior prejudice, inclination, or disposition," and specifically that these "free will" choices are not ultimately predestined by God.**

According to the Bible, the choices of man are not only ultimately determined by the sovereignty of God, but morally determined by one's nature. Man is indeed a free moral agent and freely makes choices, but in his natural state he necessarily acts in accordance with his fallen nature. Man willingly makes choices that flow from the heart, and sin is also always attributed to the desires of the heart" (James 1:13-15).[27]

This philosophy of thought raises another historic question of high debate. If the choice of right and wrong, good and evil; God and the Devil had not been given to man, would life for him been easier?

Of course the answer is yes. Life would have been easier because man would not have to think and only good would have been around us and the universe would be without sin and shame. Yes, "God could have eliminated all evil in the design of His universe. However, such a universe would have been unable to accomplish the main purpose for which God created the universe in the first place - **to allow free will choice by human beings.**

God has designed the laws of the universe so that human beings are unable to exhibit unlimited amounts of evil. However, it is not possible to design a universe in which the exercise of evil is completely eliminated, since evil begins in the minds of human beings.

To restrict the minds of human beings is to turn them into robots. Although this approach might seem attractive (especially for some people we know), it would prevent people from expressing true love - for each other and for God their Creator. [30]

Once again, when faced with the difficult dilemmas presented by the Devil and the flesh, "what do I do?" In the book of Romans, Paul described his wrestling match with the flesh. He said, "We know that the law is spiritual; but I am unspiritual, sold as a slave to sin.

I do not understand what I do. For what I want to do, I do not do, but what I hate, I do. And if I do what I do not want to do, I agree that the law is good. As it is, it is no longer I myself who do it, but it is sin living in me. I know that nothing good lives in me, that is, in my sinful nature.

For I have the desire to do what is good; but I cannot carry it out. For what I do is not the good I want to do; no, the evil I do not want to do--this I keep on doing. Now if I do what I do not want to do, it is no longer I who do it, but it is sin living in me that does it.

So I find this law at work: When I want to do good, evil is right there with me. For in my inner being I delight in God's law; but I see another law at work in the members of my body, waging war against the law of my mind and making me a prisoner of the law of sin at work within my members.

What a wretched man I am! Who will rescue me from this body of death? Thanks be to God--through Jesus Christ our Lord! So then, I myself in my mind (or higher nature, WMS) am a slave to God's law, but in the sinful (Or lower) nature a slave to the law of sin" (Roman 7: 14-25 NIV).

Paul seems to be suggesting that man naturally sins, even when he knows what is right, he still does wrong. The question must be examined, why does he do it? The answer seems to reside within each one of us. It seems that man was created to relate to God because of the God breath that was breathed into him (as discussed earlier).

But he was born also to relate to the earthly things because he was made from the earth (dirt). Because of his natural creative substance, his fleshly nature is called the natural man (from nature).

With the breath of God in man, he is a walking Spirit with a soul. In the flesh (the natural man) he is able to make decisions by way of the Free Will that God gave to him. To further define the differences, all of the following applies to the natural man:

1. Operates On Human Wisdom
The natural man may be defined as an individual who operates entirely on human wisdom: (Which is in direct opposition to the commands of God. The wisdom of Solomon directs us to "Trust in the LORD with all your heart and lean not on your own understanding; in all your ways acknowledge him, and he will make your paths straight. Do not be wise in your own eyes; fear the LORD and shun evil" (Pro. 3: 5-6 NIV).

This is due to the fact that the natural man has not made a commitment to Jesus Christ. They have not experienced the new birth and do not have the Holy Spirit living on the inside of them.

Because the natural man does not have the Spirit of God living in them, they do not understand or welcome spiritual truth. It is foolishness unto them. The unbeliever cannot understand how a person who died almost 2000 years ago can have any meaning with the way they are living today.

2. No Real Understanding Of Bible
They do not receive or welcome the message of Scripture. Their reaction to the message of the gospel is that it is foolishness and ridiculous.

3. Does Not Have The Proper Equipment
Unsaved humanity does not have the proper equipment to make proper estimate of spiritual truth. As stars are telescopically discerned, and germs are microscopically discerned, the Bible is discerned by the Holy Spirit. It would be like a blind person judging an art contest.

Many sincere and educated people admire the Bible as literature and extol its moral teaching—but they miss the real spiritual message of the Bible that salvation is only through the person of Jesus Christ.

4. Miss the Purpose
These same people may acknowledge Christ as a wonderful teacher or example but they miss the real purpose of why He came into the world. Paul wrote. Here is a trustworthy saying that deserves full acceptance: Christ Jesus came into the world to save sinners, of whom I am the worst" (I Timothy 1:15). [29]

To further define the Spirit man the following applies, which the opposite of the natural man:

1. Operates on spiritual wisdom.

2. Accepts the word of the Bible.

3. Operates with the right equipment.

4. Understands the purpose.

The important point here is to realize that everyone is born as a natural human being ruled by flesh and blood (born in sin and shaped in iniquity). The Psalmist said it this way," Surely I was sinful at birth, sinful from the time my mother conceived me" Psalm 51: 5 NIV).

But in Eph. 4: 23-24, "You were taught, with regard to your former way of life, to put off your old self, which is being corrupted by its deceitful desires; to be made new in the attitude of your minds; and to put on the new self, created to be like God in true righteousness and holiness" (Eph. 4. 23-24 NIV).

We are instructed to put on the new man, which is the spiritual man because in Romans 8: 5-9, "Those who live according to the sinful nature have their minds set on what that nature desires; but those who live in accordance with the Spirit have their minds set on what the Spirit desires.

The mind of sinful man is death, but the mind controlled by the Spirit is life and peace; the sinful mind is hostile to God. It does not submit to God's law, nor can it do so. Those controlled by the sinful nature cannot please God.

You, however, are controlled not by the sinful nature but by the Spirit, if the Spirit of God lives in you. And if anyone does not have the Spirit of Christ, he does not belong to Christ. But if Christ is in you, your body is dead because of sin, yet your spirit is alive because of righteousness. And if the Spirit of him who raised Jesus from the dead is living in you, he who raised Christ from the dead will also give life to your mortal bodies through his Spirit, who lives in you" (Eph. 8: 5-11 NIV).

"The man without the Spirit does not accept the things that come from the Spirit of God, for they are foolishness to him, and he cannot understand them, because they are spiritually discerned" (I Cor. 2: 14 NIV). The question is, how do I change? The book has an answer for you. Your soul is longing to be connected to God. You know that something s missing. You are familiar with the term, "walking dead man."

Your spirit is dead; wanting to be awakened by God. Remember the term Free Will, you must choose to renew your mind and retrain the flesh. You are destined to become the spiritual being that God created you to be. Accept the Bible, operate in wisdom and use the right equipment and understand what Christ came to do in your life.

The word says, "The acts of the sinful nature are obvious: sexual immorality, impurity and debauchery; idolatry and witchcraft; hatred, discord, jealousy, fits of rage, selfish ambition, dissensions, factions and envy; drunkenness, orgies, and the like.

I warn you, as I did before, that those who live like this will not inherit the kingdom of God. But the fruit of the Spirit is love, joy, peace, patience, kindness, goodness, faithfulness, gentleness and self-control. Against such things there is no law" (Gal. 5: 17-21 NIV).

A word about Biblical Humanity: There are certain inherent understandings about human nature in the biblical view: (l) each person is a unique individual- (s) he has the power to act under his/her own initiative; (2) as a whole, mankind is a good creation of God, firmly tied to the finite world, but with the important qualifications of dominion and stewardship, a freedom to move within the limits of time and space, and to affect the course of history;

(3) The real criteria for the exercise of that freedom is its correspondence to the will and intention of God - there are right and wrong modes of conduct. In substance, these considerations make one aspect about mankind central to biblical religion:

By design, human beings are in *relation*. They are in relation to their environment, to God, to their neighbors, and to the larger human community. This is a natural consequence of each person's status as a personal being. Women and men enter into contact with events, objects, and characters surrounding them. Moreover, as noted by Wright, "The central fact about the place of man in creation according to the Old Testament is the dignity and honor accorded him by God." Elsewhere it has been noted:

In the Bible, the individual is in a special relationship to the Creator. Human uniqueness lies not chiefly in our reason or in our relationship to nature. Instead, each person is a worthwhile, unique individual created by God. Human beings are regarded...as made "in the image of God"; that is, the Creator has endowed us with unique attributes of a free agent capable of love, characteristics analogous to God's own self-expression.

The Biblical image of the human soul is distinctly different: it is God's gift. God has made man as inherently good, in God's own image, *i.e.*, with the ability to act, to make decisions, and enter into relation. The logical extension of this interpretation is that the human soul, through an act of God's grace, remains uniquely human, though not necessarily mortal.

According to biblical religion, "The soul is not an entity with a separate nature from the flesh and possessing or capable of a life of its own (in the material). Rather it is the life animating the flesh." By way of elaboration, others have noted:

Nephesh means primarily "breath." (It) is often used also with the meaning "living being," human or otherwise. In Gen. 2:7 the first man became a living *nephesh* when Yahweh's breath (a different word) was breathed into his nostrils. Frequently the best translation of the word is "person." Clearly the word "soul" in the Bible has a much broader meaning than in current use now. One might also say that a human being is a "breather."

Man is a living soul. This sentence, which corresponds easily to Gen. 2:7, says three things: It says first of all that man became a living soul and now is a living soul. It does not say that man *has* a living soul. Soul is the nature of man, not his possession. The second thing that the sentence says is that man is a soul. Were man only flesh made from the dust he would be only body. Were man only spirit without body, he would be formless.

The third implication, according to Kohler, is that man has a body, for "Form is essential to the soul." The famous verse in Genesis (2:7) does not say, as is often supposed, that man consists of body and soul; it says that Yahweh shaped man, earth from the ground, and then proceeded to animate the inert figure with living breath blown into his nostrils, so that man became a living *being*, which is all that *nephesh* here means.

The important thing here is the conception of man as body, not as soul or spirit. The Hebrew idea of human personality is an animated body, not an incarnated soul.

The soul, therefore, is a functioning, integrated aspect of human nature and of behavior. It represents that part of human consciousness which moves toward fellowship with God. This is not, however, a union of like parts, of the fragment returning to the whole, but rather two individual identities joining together in positive relation, in communion.

The soul can then be spoken of as being active, not as the prisoner of the body, but as its animating conscience. It enters into human activity, directing that action by offering up possibilities which correspond to the will of God.[28]

Make note: this report is not about what man "says" or even "think" is the reason that he does what he does. The report is about, why he "really" does what he does. Obviously, within this statement there is an implication that man will "say" or "think" one thing; and mean another.

To summarize the evidence: There are a few things that need to be recapped. First, the jury has made its ruling that the Devil is real and attempting every day to influence humanity toward confusion and destruction. Meanwhile the foreman of the jury makes a fact finding report as well. The Devil can NOT make man do anything.

Also, the jury has found that God is real. In the report of history on God (which is a little different from the report on the Devil), it is substantiated that God does have the power to force man to follow his directions.

Although God has the power and the desire for man to follow his direction; God will not force man because of the gift of Free Will that He has given him. Having given that brief summary, the conversation that now stands, knocking at the front door is, why do I (mankind) really do what I do?

After all that has been said about Satan, it should not surprise anyone that has read the book up to this point that out of all of the personalities who have contributed to the discussion, Satan would be the one in the book of Job, to raise the question about mankind's motive.

Since the "Fall," mankind needs to acknowledge that his flesh was corrupted; Along with other certain facts of change. He certainly needs to admit that he is not the same creature that he was before. With corrupted flesh and with-out the morality of the God that created him in his image and likeness, mankind has a serious dilemma. Literally, he is in a life and death situation.

The desires of the flesh are real and everyday of man's existence, he's challenged by them. Jesus said to Nicodemus, "What is born of the flesh is flesh, and what is born of the Spirit is spirit. Do not be astonished that I said to you, 'You must be born from above" (John 3: 6 NRSV).

Additionally, along with his natural tendencies to follow the flesh into self satisfaction; mankind has the Devil and his demons whispering evil into his ear. Although this is bad news, but there is some good news. Mankind has the God of the Universe whispering into his other ear. The answer to the great question of the book, "**why I really do what**

I do" is this: What I do is still up to me. It is still my choice and my choice alone!

As Joshua said, "But if serving the LORD seems undesirable to you, then choose for yourselves this day whom you will serve, whether the gods your forefathers served beyond the River, or the gods of the Amorites, in whose land you are living. But as for me and my household, we will serve the LORD." Then the people answered, "Far be it from us to forsake the LORD to serve other gods!

It was the LORD our God himself who brought us and our fathers up out of Egypt, from that land of slavery, and performed those great signs before our eyes. He protected us on our entire journey and among all the nations through which we traveled. And the LORD drove out before us all the nations, including the Amorites, who lived in the land. We too will serve the LORD, because he is our God."

Joshua said to the people, "You are not able to serve the LORD. He is a holy God; he is a jealous God. He will not forgive your rebellion and your sins. If you forsake the LORD and serve foreign gods, he will turn and bring disaster on you and make an end of you, after he has been good to you." But the people said to Joshua, "No! We will serve the LORD" (Joshua 24: 15-21 NIV).

Ultimately, then why I do what I really do is my choice! Under the influence of the Devil, yes: Under the influence of God, yes: Even under the influence of my nature which has been corrupted toward the Devil's desires, yes. But the choice is still mine to decide what I do. Therefore we must remind ourselves of these facts each and every day, if we are to defeat the Devil and live successful and happy lives.

Remember the exhortation of John the beloved disciple, **"I write to you, children, because you know the Father. I write to you, fathers, because you know him who is from the beginning. I write to you, young people, because you are strong and the word of God abides in you, and you have overcome the Evil One.**

Do not love the world or the things in the world. The love of the Father is not in those who love the world; for all that is in the world--the desire of the flesh, the desire of the eyes, the pride in riches--comes not from the Father but from the world. And the world and its desire are passing away, but those who do the will of God live forever" (I JOHN 2: 14-17 NRSV).

Before moving on to the next chapter, write down at least three tidbits of information learned from the above chapter.

1._____

2._____

3._____

CHAPTER IX

WHY DO THE RIGHTEOUS SUFFER?

SOME GOOD PEOPLE IN SOME BAD SITUATIONS!

1. ADAM AND EVE'S DISOBEDIENCE AND STRUGGLE WITH EVIL IN THE WORLD!
"But the LORD God called to the man, and said to him, "Where are you? He said, "I heard the sound of you in the garden, and I was afraid, because I was naked; and I hid myself." He said, "Who told you that you were naked? Have you eaten from the tree of which I commanded you not to eat?"

The man said, "The woman whom you gave to be with me, she gave me fruit from the tree, and I ate." Then the LORD God said to the woman, "What is this that you have done?" The woman said, "The serpent tricked me, and I ate." The LORD God said to the serpent, "Because you have done this, cursed are you among all animals and among all wild creatures; upon your belly you shall go, and dust you shall eat all the days of your life.

I will put enmity between you and the woman, and between your offspring and hers; he will strike your head, and you will strike his heel." To the woman he said, "I will greatly increase your pangs in childbearing; in pain you shall bring forth children, yet your desire shall be for your husband, and he shall rule over you."

And to the man he said, "Because you have listened to the voice of your wife, and have eaten of the tree about which I commanded you, 'You shall not eat of it,' cursed is the ground because of you; in toil you shall eat of it all the days of your life" (Genesis 3: 9-17 NKJV).

2. NOAH'S RIGHTEOUSNESS AND STRUGGLE WITH EVIL IN THE WORLD!

"Then the LORD said to Noah, "Go into the ark, you and all your household, for I have seen that you alone are righteous before me in this generation"(Genesis 7: 1 NKJV).

3. JOB'S RIGHTEOUSNESS AND STRUGGLE WITH EVIL IN THE WORLD!

The LORD said to Satan, "Where have you come from?" Satan answered the LORD, "From going to and fro on the earth, and from walking up and down on it." The LORD said to Satan, "Have you considered my servant Job? There is no one like him on the earth, a blameless and upright man who fears God and turns away from evil"(Job 1: 7-8 NKJV).

4. THE THREE HEBREW BELIEVERS RIGHTEOUSNESS AND STRUGGLE WITH EVIL IN THE WORLD.

"There are certain Jews whom you have appointed over the affairs of the province of Babylon: Shadrach, Meshach, and Abednego. These pay no heed to you, O King. They do not serve your gods and they do not worship the golden statue that you have set up"(Dan. 3: 12 NRSV).

5. DANIEL'S RIGHTEOUSNESS AND STRUGGLE WITH EVIL IN THE WORLD!

"Soon Daniel distinguished himself above all the other presidents and satraps because an excellent spirit was in him, and the king planned to appoint him over the whole kingdom. So the presidents and the satraps tried to find grounds for complaint against Daniel in connection with the kingdom.

But they could find no grounds for complaint or any corruption, because he was faithful, and no negligence or corruption could be found in him. The men said, "We shall not find any ground for complaint against this Daniel unless we find it in connection with the law of his God"(Dan. 6: 3-6 NRSV).

6. THE BLIND MAN'S RIGHTEOUSNESS AND STRUGGLE WITH EVIL IN THE WORLD.

"As he went along, he saw a man blind from birth. His disciples asked him, "Rabbi, who sinned, this man or his parents, that he was born blind? Neither this man nor his parents sinned, said Jesus, but this happened so that the work of God might be displayed in his life.

As long as it is day, we must do the work of him who sent me. Night is coming, when no one can work. While I am in the world, I am the light of the world. Having said this, he spit on the ground, made some mud with the saliva, and put it on the man's eyes. Go, he told him, wash in the Pool of Siloam (this word means Sent). So the man went and washed, and came home seeing"(John 9: 1-7 NIV).

7. LAZARUS RIGHTEOUSNESS AND STRUGGLE WITH EVIL IN THE WORLD!

"Now a certain man was ill, Lazarus of Bethany, the village of Mary and her sister Martha. Mary was the one who anointed the Lord with perfume and wiped his feet with her hair; her brother Lazarus was ill.

So the sisters sent a message to Jesus, "Lord, he whom you love is ill." But when Jesus heard it, he said, "This illness does not lead to death; rather it is for God's glory, so that the Son of God may be

glorified through it." Accordingly, though Jesus loved Martha and her sister and Lazarus, after having heard that Lazarus was ill, he stayed two days longer in the place where he was" (John 11: 1-5).

Up to this point in the book, there have been many great questions raised and hopefully, answered. But in the previous chapter, another great question was raised. In fact the question raised was one of the great age old questions of history. Even with all of the books written on the subject, the question, "why do the righteous suffer" is still one of great controversy.

I thank God that the Holy Spirit did not allow me to write a book on the subject of the Devil and the evil in the world and not address the question. It is a great question, "why do the righteous suffer?" Have you ever thought about it?

Why are there so many good, God fearing, every Sunday and Wednesday night church attendees; truly dedicated and saved people having so many evil experiences and treacherous occurrences in their lives? Why are the people of God attacked daily and harassed on a regular basis?

Why are they experiencing tragedies and disasters of every kind? Why do the righteous have children born with deformities? Why do the righteous' children die in automobile accidents in their youth with the majority of their lives ahead of them to live? Why in those same automobile accidents, the drunk driver lives and the innocent church going young person die?

Why do innocent children die at the hands of mass murderers, murderous parents and pedophiles living next door? Why do the young of the righteous end up killed at college by some cold hearted and callous lunatic? Why do the people that are helped when down and almost out, get up and back on their feet act like they have never been helped? Why do they have the attitude that it is not what you have done for me, but what have you done lately?

The list of why this and why that is far too long to call forth every example. Today more than ever, there are so many people asking the question; Why, Why, Why?

The question becomes more problematic for the righteous when they observed the unrighteous living lives of ease and contentment and seemingly being exempt from trouble and tragedy: The man on the job and the neighbor living next door that doesn't even drive by the church or give any thought of actually going into the church for worship. Yet they seem blessed.

The people that don't pay tithes or hardly ever give any thing of value to the church: They don't rip and run back and forth to the church or for the church's mission: They don't spend vast amounts of monies on gas or the mechanical upkeep of the automobiles used for Godly adventures. They don't sing on the choirs or serve in any capacity of the church. Yet they seem blessed.

Materially speaking, there are times when the unrighteous seem to have more going for them than the righteous: a sensitive subject for the righteous. If you want to disturb the righteous; just conversed about the prosperity of the wicked and quickly the frustration of the righteous will stand up and make its case.

The righteous already have problems with trouble and tragedy, but particularly so when the wicked appears immune. Immediately the question of injustice is raised. The righteous want to know; what's going on? How can these things be? The suggestion being; there has to be something wrong with this picture. The righteous should be blessed. It is the unrighteous that should be suffering.

To these facts, there can be no denial. This is a dilemma of the righteous and one that deserves an explanation or at the very least, a thorough examination. The first step in any examination is to strip the item being examined down to its naked core. The items of clothing or covering must be removed in order to better see the real problem.

The examination is worthless, if the object is misdiagnosed. Therefore, the clothing of tradition must go: Biblical misinterpretation and misunderstanding must be removed: the false ideologies and doctrines of history must be laid to the side.

At the heart of the examination lay the question, "why do the righteous suffer?" Therefore, righteousness must be defined and re-examined. The term must be dissected, what part does it play? Could it be that possibly goodness and righteousness or even evil and unrighteousness do not play any part in the play entitled, "Why Do the Righteous Suffer?"

The question that must be laid under the microscope of investigation is this; does righteousness present any real relevance to the question of suffering or even to the question of prosperity? Is it theologically sound, proper or valid to argue its necessity to the process and present it as a prerequisite to prosperity?

In other words, does righteousness always precede prosperity and does wickedness precede suffering and shame? If the answer is yes, it's true, then I must ask, was it Old Testament thought and law or New Testament: Or both?

Before the question can be answered or even properly addressed, there really is a prerequisite that does need research. The ideology or definition of righteousness of the Old Testament must be examined. Particularly, the era that righteousness was thought or assumed immune to evil must be investigated.

To accomplish the task at hand, the **first** obstacle to overcome is the defining of the word "righteous" during the Old Testament Period. By tradition, the **second** hurdle of defense to overcome is the misunderstanding of the New Testament teachings of the term "righteous." Possibly, there may have been changes in the term from the Old Testament times to the New Testament.

The **third** dilemma of discussion is the ideology or thought of immunity of the righteous from evil in both Testaments periods.

> **First,** the definition of righteousness: What was the criterion needed to declare a person "good" or "righteous?" In the Old Testament, the definition of righteousness included the following: persons that kept their end of the covenant (contract) between God and man.
>
> Wikipedia says it like this: "Righteousness is one of the chief attributes of <u>God</u>. Its chief meaning concerns <u>ethical</u> conduct. (E.g., <u>Leviticus</u> 19:36; <u>Deuteronomy</u> 25:1; <u>Psalm</u> 1:6; <u>Proverbs</u> 8:20). It is used in a <u>legal</u> sense; while the guilty are judged, the guiltless are deemed righteous. God's faithfulness to His <u>covenant</u> is also a large part of His righteousness" (<u>Nehemiah</u> 9:7-8).
>
> The Hebrew word for righteousness is *tseh'-dek*, tzedek, <u>Gesenius's</u> <u>Strong's Concordance</u>: 6664—righteous, integrity, equity, justice, straightness. The root of *tseh'-dek* is *tsaw-dak'*, Gesenius's Strong:6663—upright, just, straight, innocent, true, sincere. It is best understood as the product of upright, moral action in accordance with some form of divine plan." [32]

In action, righteousness of the Old Testament can be viewed in the book of Micah, chapter six. The prophet, Micah asked, "With what shall I come before the Lord, and bow myself before the high God? Shall I come before Him with burnt offerings, with calves a year old? Will the Lord be pleased with thousands of rams, ten thousand rivers of oil? Shall I give my first born for my transgression, the fruit of my body for the sin of my soul?

He hath shown you, O man, what is good; and what the Lord require of you, but to do justly, to love mercy and to walk humbly with thy God" (Micah 6: 6-8 NKJV; TD Jakes Bible). In the Old Testament, to be good and right was to do justly, love mercy and walk humbly with God. Also, the thought of the day was; those that carried out the actions of justice, mercy and humility would be blessed.

Notice the words of the first Psalm. The writer said, "Blessed is the man who does not walk in the counsel of the wicked or stand in the way of sinners or sit in the seat of mockers. But his delight is in the law of the LORD, and on his law he meditates day and night. He is like a tree planted by streams of water, which yields its fruit in season and whose leaf does not wither. **Whatever he does prospers**" (Psalm 1: 1-3 NIV).

Furthermore, to contrast the blessings of the righteous, the Psalmist continued and said, "Not so the wicked! They are like chaff that the wind blows away. Therefore the wicked will not stand in the judgment, nor sinners in the assembly of the righteous. **For the Lord watches over the way of the righteous, but the way of the wicked will perish**" (Psalm 1: 4-6 NIV).

In the Old Testament, Deut. 29, the blessings of the righteous is seen again. "Moses summoned all the Israelites and said to them: Your eyes have seen all that the LORD did in Egypt to Pharaoh, to all his officials and to all his land. With your own eyes you saw those great trials, those miraculous signs and great wonders. But to this day the LORD has not given you a mind that understands or eyes that see or ears that hear.

During the forty years that I led you through the desert, your clothes did not wear out, nor did the sandals on your feet. You ate no bread and drank no wine or other fermented drink. I did this so that you might know that I am the LORD your God. When you reached this place, Sihon king of Heshbon and Og king of Bashan came out to fight against us, but we defeated them.

We took their land and gave it as an inheritance to the Reubenites, the Gadites and the half-tribe of Manasseh. Carefully follow the terms of this covenant, **so that you may prosper in everything you do**" (Deut. 29: 2-9 NIV).

Time and time again, throughout the Old Testament, the thought of the righteous blessedness was asserted. Solomon said, "The righteous man is rescued from trouble, and it comes on the wicked instead. With his mouth the godless destroys his neighbor, but through knowledge the righteous escape.

When the righteous prosper, the city rejoices; when the wicked perish, there are shouts of joy. Through the blessing of the upright a city is exalted, but by the mouth of the wicked it is destroyed." (Proverbs 11: 8-11 NIV).

The book of Job details the ideology of Job's three friends. One of them, "Eliphaz the Temanite replied: "Consider now: Who, being innocent, has ever perished? Where were the upright ever destroyed? As I have observed, those who plow evil and those who sow trouble reap it. At the breath of God they are destroyed; at the blast of his anger they perish" (Job 4: 1; 8-9 NIV).

These are but a few of the many texts of the Bible attesting to the facts that within the Old Testament thought, the righteous were to be blessed. In fact, exegesis revealed, the righteous were blessed. Noah was blessed. The Bible says, "Then God blessed Noah and his sons, saying to them, "Be fruitful and increase in number and fill the earth.

The fear and dread of you will fall upon all the beasts of the earth and all the birds of the air, upon every creature that moves along the ground, and upon all the fish of the sea; they are given into your hands. Everything that lives and moves will be food for you. Just as I gave you the green plants, I now give you everything" (Genesis 9: 1-3 NIV).

Abraham was blessed. The Bible says, "And he blessed Abram, saying, "Blessed be Abram by God Most High, Creator of heaven and earth. And blessed be God Most High, who delivered your enemies into your hand." Then Abram gave him a tenth of everything" (Genesis 14: 19-20 NIV). He was blessed to be a blessing to others and he was. He blessed all of them that were around him, including his nephew, Lot.

Isaac was blessed. The Bible says, "Isaac planted crops in that land and the same year reaped a hundredfold, because the LORD blessed him. The man became rich, and his wealth continued to grow until he became very wealthy. He had so many flocks and herds and servants that the Philistines envied him" (Genesis 26: 12-14 NIV).

"I swear by myself, declares the LORD, that because you have done this and have not withheld your son, your only son, I will surely bless you and make your descendants as numerous as the stars in the sky and as the sand on the seashore. Your descendants will take possession of the cities of their enemies, and through your offspring all nations on earth will be blessed, because you have obeyed me" (Genesis 22: 16-18 NIV).

Joseph was blessed. The Bible says, "Then Pharaoh said to Joseph, "Since God has made all this known to you, there is no one so discerning and wise as you. You shall be in charge of my palace, and all my people are to submit to your orders. Only with respect to the throne will I be greater than you."

So Pharaoh said to Joseph, "I hereby put you in charge of the whole land of Egypt." Then Pharaoh took his signet ring from his finger and put it on Joseph's finger. He dressed him in robes of fine linen and put a gold chain around his neck" (Genesis 41: 40-42 NIV).

1. There was no question that the thought of the day was; the righteous would be blessed for their righteousness. As stated and they were blessed for being righteous in the Old Testament. Further, it was said that Abraham was blessed for not withholding his only son from the altar of sacrifice. He was truly righteous. The question for the New Testament Christian is, can we claim that kind of righteousness today?

2. Notice that the Old Testament saint's reward for righteousness was **physical and material: long life and prosperity.** God said to Moses,

   "But you stay here with me so that I may give you all the commands, decrees and laws you are to teach them to follow in the land I am giving them to possess."

   So be careful to do what the LORD your God has commanded you; do not turn aside to the right or to the left. Walk in all the way that the LORD your God has commanded you, so that you may live and prosper and prolong your days in the land that you will possess" (Deut. 5: 31-33 NIV).

   The New Testament saint's promises for being righteous include the physical and material, but extend beyond that. They include everlasting life through Christ, Jesus our Lord. Jesus said, "But strive first for the kingdom of God and his righteousness, and all these things will be given to you as well" (Matt. 6: 33 NRSV).

3. Exegesis reveals something well worth consideration. The Old Testament saint's prosperity was material blessings. Yet, it did not prohibit evil or trial and tribulation. Although, it must be accurately reported that apparently, many people during the time thought that prosperity included immunity from trouble.

   Obviously, this was an error of judgment because it did not. The life experiences of the righteous men and women like Noah, Abraham, Isaac, Jacob, Joseph, Moses, Joshua, Jeremiah, Ezekiel, Isaiah, Daniel, the three Hebrew believers, Deborah, Queen Esther and many others all testify that the prosperity of the righteous did not immune them from trouble. Neither did it immune Jesus Christ our

Lord. They all had trouble because of the presence of evil in the world.

The Old Testament righteous had trouble, trials and tribulations as we have in the New Testament. In this area, nothing has changed much in the requirements of God. Again, the **second** hurdle of defense to overcome is the misunderstanding of the New Testament teachings of the term "righteous." The New Testament righteousness still requires man to live by what he believes and confesses.

However, there is one major difference; the observation of righteousness in the New Testament now includes faith in Christ and the Holy Spirit as well as in God. In the Old Testament, righteousness was predicated upon human's obedience. In the New Testament, righteousness is predicated upon the obedience of Christ.

In the Old Testament, man failed in his attempt to be righteous. Adam and Eve failed and after the Ten Commandments were given, man failed to keep them. These failures of mankind created the necessity of Jesus Christ.

However today, when men and women obtain righteousness, they are declared so because of the righteousness of Christ. This is what Paul was referring to in the letter to the Romans. He said, "For, being ignorant of the righteousness that comes from God, and seeking to establish their own, they have not submitted to God's righteousness.

For, Christ is the end of the law; so that there may be righteousness for everyone who believes. Moses writes concerning the righteousness that comes from the law, that "the person who does these things will live by them. But the righteousness that comes from faith says, "Do not say in your heart, 'Who will ascend into heaven? (that is, to bring Christ down) "or 'Who will descend into the abyss? (that is, to bring Christ up from the dead).

But what does it say? "The word is near you, on your lips and in your heart" (that is, the word of faith that we proclaim); because if you confess with your lips that Jesus is Lord and believe in your heart that God raised him from the dead, you will be saved" (Roman 10 3-9 NKJV).

From all that has been exegeted and presented in this chapter, we have learned that there are at least three kinds of suffering: Suffering as a result of our own doing, suffering as a result of God allowing us to be tested for his glory and suffering just because there is evil in the world.

Adam and Eve were righteous. Yet their suffering was due to their own doing. They deliberately chose to disobey God and suffered the consequences of that choice.

The Scripture says, "Do not be deceived: God cannot be mocked. A man reaps what he sows. The one who sows to please his sinful nature, from that nature will reap destruction; the one who sows to please the Spirit, from the Spirit will reap eternal life" (Gal. 6: 7-8 NIV). It needs repeating that sometimes the righteous suffer because of the bad choices they made.

The third dilemma of dissolution in the discussion is the ideology of immunity of goodness and righteousness from evil and tragedy. It is a serious theological misunderstanding because as has been repeatedly demonstrated; many times good and righteous people suffer. They do so, although they have done no wrong. Sometimes God allows the righteous to suffer as a test for a testimony.

THE BLIND MAN'S DILEMMA!

At other times, God allowed them to suffer for the cause of God and His glory. John recorded, "As he walked along, he saw a man blind from birth. His disciples asked him, "Rabbi, who sinned, this man or his parents, that he was born blind? Jesus answered, "Neither this man nor his parents sinned; he was born blind so that God's works might be revealed in him. We must work the works of him who sent me while it is day; night is coming when no one can work" (John 9: 1-4 NRSV).

NOAH'S DILEMMA!

Another such story is detailed in the sixth chapter of the book of Genesis. The Bible says, "This is the account of Noah. Noah was a righteous man, blameless among the people of his time, and he walked with God" (Genesis 6: 9 NIV).

Noah was declared righteous by God and yet Noah suffered. The Bible declared Noah to be 500 years old when God spoke to him about building the ark for an oncoming flood (Genesis 5: 32 & 6: 13-14). He was 600 years old when the flood waters came upon the earth (Genesis 7: 6).

I have been told that Noah preached for 120 years about an oncoming flood, yet the Scripture indicated that it was 100 years. However, for 100 years or so, Noah endured the wrath of man concerning his project to build the ark, when it had never rained upon the earth.

He endured criticism, mocking and some serious harassment and pain from the people of his day. He suffered consistently at their hands for about one hundred years or so. The question is; why did Noah suffer? He was an undisputed righteous man?

THE THREE HEBREW BELIEVER'S DILEMMA!

The book of Daniel reveals the struggle of three Hebrew believers. The book says, "They do not serve your gods and they do not worship the golden statue that you have set up" (Dan. 3: 12b NRSV). The three believers suffered ridicule, jealousy and envy. They were brought before the king for destruction because of their righteousness. To escape the fiery furnace, all they needed to do was bow and serve another god other than Jehovah.

Their response to the king's threats was historic and need to be epitomized. The Bible says, "Shadrach, Meshach, and Abednego answered the king, "O Nebuchadnezzar, we have no need to present a defense to you in this matter. If our God whom we serve is able to deliver us from the furnace of blazing fire and out of your hand, O king, let him deliver us.

But if not, be it known to you, O king, that we will not serve your gods and we will not worship the golden statue that you have set up" (Dan. 3: 16-18 NRSV). As a result of their response, they were throne into the fiery furnace. The question is, why did they suffer? Although, for those that are not familiar with the story, they were delivered. Yet why did they have to go through all of the trials and tribulation? They were righteous men.

DANIEL'S DILEMMA!

Daniel was a righteous man. The fact that his enemies could not find any error or sin in his life is a testimony of his righteousness. The Bible says, "So the presidents and the satraps tried to find grounds for complaint against Daniel in connection with the kingdom.

But they could find no grounds for complaint or any corruption, because he was faithful, and no negligence or corruption could be found in him. The men said, "We shall not find any ground for complaint against this Daniel unless we find it in connection with the law of his God" (Dan. 6: 4-5 NRSV).

But despite Daniel's righteousness, he was cast into a lions den. Although delivered, he spent all of the night surrounded by hungry, ferocious lions.

Why was Daniel disliked and talked negatively about? Why was his life put in jeopardy? Clearly he was a righteous man.

JOB'S DILEMMA!

The book of Job details the predicament of another righteous man. The LORD said to Satan, "Where have you come from?" Satan answered the LORD, "From going to and fro on the earth, and from walking up and down on it." The LORD said to Satan, "Have you considered my servant Job? There is no one like him on the earth, a blameless and upright man who fears God and turns away from evil"(Job 1: 7-8 NKJV).

There can be no real debate concerning the righteousness of Job, for God personally declared his status. He said to Satan, "there is none like Job on the face of the earth, a blameless and upright man who fears God and turns away from evil." Yet Job suffered tremendously.

The book detailed Job's tremendous loss. He loss seven thousand sheep: Three thousand camels: Five hundred yoke of oxen: Five hundred she asses and a very great household of servants. Job even loss his seven sons and three daughters; the fairest in the land. In reality, Job loss his wife as well. She told him to curse God and die" (Job 2: 9) Job loss it all.

Concerning the belief (or thought of the day) that the righteous were immune from evil, the book of Job verified it directly. The Bible says, "Then Bildad the Shuhite replied: "How long will you say such things? Your words are a blustering wind. Does God pervert justice? Does the Almighty pervert what is right?

When your children sinned against him, he gave them over to the penalty of their sin. But if you will look to God and plead with the Almighty, if you are pure and upright, even now he will rouse himself on your behalf and restore you to your rightful place" (Job 8: 1-6).

By looking through the windows of heaven and listening to the conversation between God and the Devil, we know that Job had not sinned. In fact, it was his righteousness that placed him into the predicament that he was in (See Job 1).

Thereby, emphatically, we know that suffering is not **always** caused by sin (although sometimes it is, as demonstrated in the situation of Adam and Eve and others in the Biblical account). But clearly it was thought so in Job's day. So, again the question is raised, why did Job suffer? We know that he was a righteous man because God declared him so.

LAZARUS' DILEMMA!

Lazarus, the brother of Martha and Mary too was a righteous man. John 11 says, He was loved by Jesus and considered his friend. Lazarus was such a friend to Jesus that at his death (although Jesus knew that He would raise him from the dead), still wept (John 11: 35). It was written in the Scripture that Lazarus suffered and died, even though Jesus could have saved him.

The Scripture says, "After having heard that Lazarus was ill, he stayed two days longer in the place where he was"(John 11: 6 NRSV). He did not immediately respond to Lazarus' suffering. This is an important fact; he did not rush to Lazarus bedside and heal him, but deliberately waited for two more days to pass. Why did Jesus allow this righteous man to suffer? He was an undisputed righteous man.

In Lazarus' situation of suffering, Jesus did not place us in suspension and neither will I. Also, there is no need for speculation; Jesus tells us the reason for Lazarus' infliction. He said, "This was done for the glory of God" (John 11: 4 KJV). The Revised Standard Version said it this way: "it is for God's glory so that God's Son may be glorified through it." The short answers to the questions, why do the righteous suffer and why there are some good people in some bad situations are as follows:

1. Adam and Eve reminds us that some suffering is due to bad choices; "we reap whatsoever we sow." If we want good crops to grow, we must plant good seeds. If we want apples, we must plant apple seeds to grow apple trees.

    The great Albert Switzer once said, "The people that keep doing the same things and expect different results are insane." We must remember that God loves and rebukes us for our sins just as parents love and rebuke their children. Hopefully, the result will be good fruit.

2. Noah, the three Hebrew believers and Daniel all remind us that sometimes suffering is the result of the presence of evil

in the world while performing the will of God. Not only is there evil in the world, there are evil people (or should I say, there are people filled with evil, malice and jealousy) in the world.

See Luke 22: 3, for an example that the Devil will enter the human body and use it for his destructive purposes. As has already been explained, God could have removed the Devil and evil from the arena of man's existence; but chose to allow their presence for his own purpose. Maybe his purpose is to bring forth the fruit of patience, faith and Christian maturity.

Another point of consideration is, this kind of faithful suffering silences the Devil. The Devil boasted that Job served God because of material blessings; yet in the end, Job proved that he loved God because of who God is.

3. Job reminds us that sometimes suffering is simply brought upon us by the Devil conspiring against us. Consistently, he goes to and fro in the earth and seeking whom he may devour. In Job, he was shown sending fire down from heaven and setting Jobs fields on fire. He was shown sending a whirlwind to the celebration at Job's children house and blowing it down, killing all ten of the children.

4. Both Lazarus **and the blind man** remind us that sometimes suffering is allowed because God's" will" must be done for God's own glory. After all, God is the Creator of the Universe and has the right to exercise control over his creation. "In the beginning, God created the heaven and the earth" (Gen. 1: 1 KJV).

The Psalmist said, "The earth is the Lord's and all that is in it, the world, and those who live in it; for he has founded it on the seas, and established it on the rivers" (Psalm 24: 1-2 NKJV).

This kind of suffering is allowed by God, both to teach us to trust and depend upon Him and enlarge our ministry by being faithful witnesses before the world. It is proven that those who have suffered themselves have a deeper understanding for the suffering.

Ezekiel said, "Then I came to them of the captivity at Telabib, that dwelt by the river of Chebar, and I sat where they sat, and remained there astonished among them seven days" (Ezek. 3: 15 KJV. After sitting where they sat, Ezekiel better understood their plight.

In all of the examples cited above dealing with mankind's suffering, there are several facts note worthy of highlighting for mankind's encouragement. First, in all of the situations, **God was well aware of every detail.** The second observation worthy of note: **God was present in each occurrence.**

The third observation: **God has the power to change each situation at any time, but allowed the suffering event to occur.** He did it in order to rebuke us, produce good fruit or to increased faith, patience and Christian maturity. In Job's case, he did it to silence the Devil.

Cited in the above examples is total concurrence with Greek thought and understanding about God's attributes: Omniscience (All Knowing), Omnipotence (All Power) and Omnipresence (All Presence).

Also, the Scriptures line up in full support of the same facts about God's attributes. Concerning God's Omniscience, Ezekiel said, "He asked me, "Son of man, can these bones live?" I said, "O Sovereign LORD, you alone know" (Ezek. 37: 3 NIV).

Concerning God's Omnipotence, Matthew said, "And Jesus came and spake unto them, saying, All power is given unto me in heaven and in earth" (Matt. 28: 18 KJV). Concerning his Omnipresence, the Psalmist said, "Where can I go from your spirit? Or where can I flee from your presence? If I ascend to heaven, you are there; if I make my bed in Sheol, you are there.

If I take the wings of the morning and settle at the farthest limits of the sea, even there your hand shall lead me, and your right hand shall hold me fast.

If I say, "Surely the darkness shall cover me, and the light around me become night," even the darkness is not dark to you; the night is as bright as the day, for darkness is as light to you" (Psalm 139: 7-12 NIV). In summary of the question, "why do the righteous suffer," the question itself could use some reconsideration and reframing. Maybe the question should ask; why do people suffer? It must be noted that the devil and evil, trouble and tragedy, death and destruction do not discriminate.

Each and every human that reside in the earth, no matter the color, race, creed or sex will be attacked. Without discrimination, the righteous and the unrighteous are mistreated the same. The Devil does not play favorites.

In fact, Jesus warned us in what really is the Lord's Prayer, recorded by John. Jesus prayed, "While I was with them, I protected them in your name that you have given me. I guarded them, and not one of them was lost except the one destined to be lost, so that the scripture might be fulfilled.

But now I am coming to you, and I speak these things in the world so that they may have my joy made complete in themselves. I have given them your word, and the world has hated them because they do not belong to the world, just as I do not belong to the world. I am not asking you to take them out of the world, but I ask you to protect them from the evil one" (John 17: 12-15).

In conclusion, **first,** the righteous suffer because of evil. **Second,** they suffer because of the Evil One (Devil). **Third,** they suffer because of man's nature or his natural desire to fulfill the lusts of the flesh.

There is no question that the world would be a better place to live, if mankind would follow the spirit of God and deny the flesh. Jesus said so: "Then Jesus told his disciples, "If any want to become my followers, let them deny themselves and take up their cross and follow me. For those who want to save their life will lose it, and those who lose their life for my sake will find it.

For what will it profit them if they gain the whole world but forfeit their soul (life or personhood)? Or what will they give in return for their life? "For the Son of Man is to come with his angels in the glory of his Father, and then he will repay everyone for what has been done. Truly I tell you, there are some standing here who will not taste death before they see the Son of Man coming in his kingdom" (Matt. 16: 24-28) NKJV).

If mankind is going to defeat the Devil (or the evil one); he must take control of his flesh? He must realize as did Jesus, the state of his condition. Jesus said, "Watch and pray, that ye enter not into temptation: the spirit indeed is willing, but the flesh is weak" (Matt. 26:41 NIV). (Stay tuned to chapter nine for the <u>HELPFUL HINTS ON HOW TO DEFEAT THE DEVIL!</u>

But before moving on to the next chapter, write down at least three tidbits of information learned from the above chapter.

1._____

2._____

3._____

CHAPTER X
HELPFUL HINTS ON HOW TO DEFEAT THE DEVIL!

"**Finally, be strong in the Lord and in the strength of his power. Put on the whole armor of God, so that you may be able to stand against the wiles of the devil. For our struggle is not against enemies of blood and flesh, but against the rulers, against the authorities, against the cosmic powers of this present darkness, against the spiritual forces of evil in the heavenly places.**

Therefore take up the whole armor of God, so that you may be able to withstand on that evil day, and having done everything, to stand firm" (Ephesians 6: 10-13, NRSV).

There is not a human being on the earth, even one as strong as Sampson that can successfully defeat the Devil and resist his influence (without God's assistance). Concerning defeating the Devil, there are at least seven lessons well worth noting in Sampson's struggle to be the best that he could be. Again as strong as he was, he needed God.

Lesson #1: All humans need God. Jesus said, "**for without me, you can do nothing**" **(John 15: 5 KJV).** Within the story of Sampson and Delilah, it was noted that Sampson was a special child for a special mission. The Scripture says, "**The angel of the LORD appeared to**

her (his Mother) and said, "You are sterile and childless, but you are going to conceive and have a son.

Now see to it that you drink no wine or other fermented drink and that you do not eat anything unclean, because you will conceive and give birth to a son. No razor may be used on his head, because the boy is to be a Nazarite, set apart to God from birth, and he will begin the deliverance of Israel from the hands of the Philistine"(Judges 13: 3-5 NIV).

"A Nazarite was an Israelite that consecrated him/herself and took a vow of separation and self imposed abstinence for the purpose of some special service."[35]Note that Sampson's mother had been told by an angel to drink no wine or strong drink while carrying Sampson.

Lesson # 2: Drinking wine and strong drink is never an advantage. Peter said, **"Be sober, be vigilant; because your adversary the devil, as a roaring lion, walketh about, seeking whom he may devour: Whom resist stedfast in the faith, knowing that the same afflictions are accomplished in your brethren that are in the world"** (I Peter. 5: 8 KJV).

"When Abigail went to Nabal, he was in the house holding a banquet like that of a king. He was in high spirits and very drunk. So she told him nothing until daybreak. Then in the morning, when Nabal was sober, his wife told him all these things, and his heart failed him and he became like a stone. About ten days later, the LORD struck Nabal and he died" (I Samuel 25: 36-38 NIV).

Paul said this: **"But now I am writing you that you must not associate with anyone who calls himself a brother; but is sexually immoral or greedy, an idolater or a slanderer, a drunkard or a swindler. With such a man do not even eat"** (I Cor. 5: 11 NIV). He also said, **"For by the grace given me I say to every one of you: Do not think of yourself more highly than you ought, but rather think of yourself** with sober judgment, in accordance with the measure of faith God has given you" (Romans 12: 3 NIV).

"Therefore let us not sleep, as do others; but let us watch and be sober. For they that sleep, sleep in the night; and they that be drunken are drunken in the night. But, let us, who are of the day, be sober; putting on the breastplate of faith and love; and for a helmet; the hope of salvation" (I Thess. 5: 6-8 NIV). On the subject of drunkenness, the Scriptures speak for themselves. Additionally, once born; due to a Nazarite's vow and commitment to God, Sampson, was not to have a razor on his head.

Lesson # 3: Men and women on God's mission must be totally committed to God. Paul said, "Therefore, I urge you, brothers, in view of God's mercy, to offer your bodies as living sacrifices, holy and pleasing to God--this is your spiritual act of worship" (Romans 12: 1 NIV).

As a result of the commitment, Sampson was blessed to become Israel's next deliverer. He would deliver them out of the hands of the Philistines.

Lesson # 4: Obedience is better than sacrifice. "And Samuel said, Hath the LORD as great delight in burnt offerings and sacrifices, as in obeying the voice of the LORD? Behold, to obey is better than sacrifice, and to hearken than the fat of rams" (I Sam. 15: 22 KJV).

To shorten a very long story; out of lust for a beautiful woman, named Delilah, Sampson disobeyed God. **As did Adam with Eve, Abraham with Hagar and Ahab with Jezebel.**

Lesson # 5: Success means taking control of your lusts, they will get you into serious trouble. James said, "Blessed is the man that endureth temptation: for when he is tried, he shall receive the crown of life, which the Lord hath promised to them that love him.

Let no man say when he is tempted, I am tempted of God: for God cannot be tempted with evil, neither tempteth he any man: But every man is tempted, when he is drawn away of his own lust and enticed. Then when lust hath conceived, it bringeth forth sin: and sin, when it is finished, bringeth forth death" (James 1: 14 KJV).

The text of James completely characterizes the life of Sampson. He lusted, he was enticed; and sinned, which brought forth his death. Out of lust, he told Delilah the source of his strength. He mistook her friendship and confided in her the secret of his blessings from God. He told her that his strength was in his hair; she put a razor on his head and cut it off. At that moment, as warned by the angel, he lost his strength and became "as a normal man."

Lesson # 6: Don't put your trust in men and women and know your friends. Don't make the mistake of Sampson and Job. Job's three friends were suspect and falsely accused him (Job 3: 1).

Solomon said, **"Trust in the LORD with all thine heart; and lean not unto thine own understanding. In all thy ways acknowledge him, and he shall direct thy paths. Be not wise in thine own eyes: fear the LORD, and depart from evil" (Proverbs 3: 5-7 KJV).**

However, one point needs clarification, Sampson's strength was not in his hair. It was in his covenant with God and was not to be broken. By disobeying God, he broke it and God left him. To make matters worse, Sampson did not know that God had left him. That lack of knowledge would eventually cost him his life.

Lesson # 7: Stay close to God. The Scripture says, **"Draw near to God, and he will draw near to you"** (James 4: 8 NRSV).

Today, my prayer to God for you the reader of the book is that you are living close enough to God to know immediately when he leaves the scene: Or better yet, when you leave him. Jesus promised to never leave the believer, He said, "Lo I will be with you always, even unto the end of the world. Amen." (Matt. 28: 20b KJV).

Again, God's presence is crucial because "without God, we can do nothing" (John 15: 5 KJV). Sampson lost contact with God and was taken captive and blinded by his enemies (Judges 13). Therefore one of the keys to overcoming the devil is to make note of the seven lessons learned above and draw near to God, Christ and the Holy Spirit and stay there.

The Apostle Paul says, "Finally, be strong in the Lord and in the strength of his power. Put on the whole armor of God, so that you may be able to stand against the wiles of the devil. For our struggle is not against enemies of blood and flesh, but against the rulers, against the authorities, against the cosmic powers of this present darkness, against the spiritual forces of evil in the heavenly places.

Therefore take up the whole armor of God, so that you may be able to withstand on that evil day, and having done everything, to stand firm" (Ephesians 6: 10-13, NRSV).

There is some specific spiritual armor that God makes available to man. He compares the defense of God's servants against Satan's influence to a "belt of truth around your waist" and a "breastplate of righteousness." He describes their combat shoes as "whatever will make you ready to proclaim the gospel of peace." Their shield is their faith in God and His Son, Jesus Christ, "with which you will be able to quench all the flaming arrows of the evil one.

Additionally, they are protected by "the helmet of salvation" (verse 17)—the assurance that in steadfastly serving and pleasing God they will receive eternal life. The one offensive weapon they have to attack Satan's attitudes and ideologies is the "sword of the Spirit, which is the word of God."

He advises us to "pray in the Spirit at all times, in every prayer and supplication. In other words, stay alert and always persevere in supplication for all of the saints" (verse 18). These are some of the keys elements for fighting off Satan attempts to control the Christian, "the ones who have escaped from those who live in error" (2 Peter 2:18).

The goal is to become more like Christ in character. Paul said, "Let this mind be in you, which was also in Christ Jesus: Who, being in the form of God, thought it not robbery to be equal with God: But made himself of no reputation, and took upon him the form of a servant, and was made in the likeness of men" (Phil 2: 5-7 KJV). To defeat the Devil we must use the methodology of Christ.

Once again, James says, this is easily achievable, "if you draw near to God, he will draw near to you" (James 4: 8). The closer we are to Christ, the more uncomfortable the Devil feels in our presence. As we know; he is very uncomfortable in the presence of God.

Mark 5 demonstrates this. "And he cried with a loud voice, and said, what have I to do with thee, Jesus, thou Son of the most high God? I adjure thee by God, that thou torment me not. For, he said unto him, Come out of the man, thou unclean spirit" (Mark 5: 7-8 KJV). Also remember, James said, "Resist the devil and he will flee from you" (James 4: 7 KJV).

In reality, there can be no serious discussion on the method to defeat the Devil without saying something about Jesus' victory in the wilderness of Jordan. Up to the time of the text (recorded in Matthew 4), it was the battle of the century.

The first Adam had been defeated by Satan's strategic warfare. He sinned and fell short of the glory of God. "For since death came through a human being, the resurrection of the dead has also come through a human being; for as all die in Adam, so all will be made alive in Christ " (I Cor. 15: 21-22 NIV).

How did Christ do it? How did he defeat the Devil? What was his methodology? To make another long story short, Christ defeated the Devil with the Word of God. Each and every temptation presented by the Devil, Christ responded with the Word of God.

Remember when Satan offered food, Christ said, "man shall not live by bread alone." When Satan offered him fame, Christ said, "Thou shall not tempt the Lord thy God." When Satan offered him power, authority and the kingdoms of the world, Christ said, "Get thee behind me, Satan: for it is written, Thou shall worship the Lord thy God, and Him only shall thou serve" (Luke 4: 8 KJV).

In Luke's gospel, Jesus told this illustration. He said, "When the unclean spirit has gone out of a person, it wanders through waterless regions looking for a resting place, but not finding any, it says, 'I will return to my house from which I came.' When it comes, it finds it swept and put in order. Then it goes and brings seven other spirits more evil than itself, and they enter and live there; and the last state of that person is worse than the first" (Luke 11: 24-26).

Briefly, the message behind the illustration is that when the Devil and his demons are overcome, the space vacated by them needs to be filled with something solid and strong. It needs to be strong enough to withstand the return of the demonic presence. The strongest fortress I know is the word of God. It worked consistently for Jesus and it will work for us. So, get in the word of God and stay there.

Once again, the first act necessary in the fight against evil is the acknowledgement of the demonic presence in the world. The second act of necessity is to acknowledge the infiltration (or the possession if you will) of demons into the human house (body). As repeatedly affirmed, the acknowledgement of demonic presence is seriously AWOL (Absence with out leave) in society; which is a major problem for the human family.

Note more closely the information of Jesus. He said, if a demon is cast out through a spiritual process (through salvation, prayer, exorcism, the laying on hands, etc), the human must fill the vacated space and replace the tenant of the house (if you will). If he doesn't the unclean spirit will return and reoccupy the house. Only this time, he will not return alone. But will return with seven other spirits and the condition of the man will be worse in the end than in the beginning.

Practically speaking, Jesus was dealing with a person that had been touched by God and trying to start fresh on a new journey with Him. The demonic presence had been removed. Specifically, the instruction from Christ was for the person to replace the demonic presence with the presence of God.

How is he to accomplish this? He must read; study and engulf the Word of God, pray, daily exercise his spirituality by listening to the preached word at every opportunity and walk with God in complete obedience. The spirit of God must be fed, nourished and made strong in preparation for the encounter with the returning demons.

Within the same chapter, note also that Jesus made this procedure more clear. He said, "When a strong man, fully armed, guards his castle, his property is safe. But when one stronger than he attacks him and overpowers him, he takes away his armor in which he trusted and divides his plunder" (Luke 11: 21-22 NRSV). Mankind can not turn his back on the Devil and afford him the opportunity to shoot him in the back because he will, without hesitation.

Finally, the question has been repeatedly asked, how can one know when the Devil is using him/her? It is a complicated question, but the easiest way to know is by the action's ones takes. The apostle Paul put it this way. He said, "For the sinful nature desires what is contrary to the Spirit, and the Spirit what is contrary to the sinful nature. They are in conflict with each other, so that you do not do what you want.

But if you are led by the Spirit, you are not under law. The acts of the sinful nature are obvious: sexual immorality, impurity and debauchery; idolatry and witchcraft; hatred, discord, jealousy, fits of rage, selfish ambition, dissensions, factions and envy; drunkenness, orgies, and the like. I warn you, as I did before, that those who live like this will not inherit the kingdom of God.

But the fruit of the Spirit is love, joy, peace, patience, kindness, goodness, faithfulness, gentleness and self-control. Against such things there is no law. Those who belong to Christ Jesus have crucified the sinful nature with its passions and desires. Since we live by the Spirit, let us keep in step with the Spirit. Let us not become conceited, provoking and envying of each other" (Gal. 5: 17-26 NIV). A person's actions speak louder than words.

In conclusion, the final Hints on how to defeat the Devil are as follows: DO NOT GIVE HIM AN INCH; HE WILL TAKE A MILE: DO NOT GIVE HIM A RIDE IN YOUR AUTOMOBILE; FOR HE WILL WANT TO DRIVE: DO NOT ALLOW HIM TO SPEND THE NIGHT; FOR HE WILL MOVE IN TOMORROW. DO NOT WALK WITH HIM; FOR HE WILL WANT YOU TO STAND WITH HIM; DO NOT STAND AND CHAT WITH HIM; FOR HE WILL WANT YOU TO SIT WITH HIM.

The Scripture put it this way. Written in the first Psalm, David said, **"Blessed is the man that WALKETH NOT in the counsel of the ungodly, nor STANDETH in the way of sinners, nor SITTETH in the seat of the scornful.**

But his delight is in the law of the LORD; and in his law doth he meditate day and night. And he shall be like a tree planted by the rivers of water, that bringeth forth his fruit in his season; his leaf also shall not wither; and whatsoever he doeth shall prosper.

The ungodly are not so: but are like the chaff which the wind driveth away. Therefore the ungodly shall not stand in the judgment,

nor sinners in the congregation of the righteous. For the LORD knoweth the way of the righteous: but the way of the ungodly shall perish" (Psalm 1: 1-6 KJV).

Remember, "Submit yourselves therefore to God. Resist the devil, and he will flee from you. Draw nigh to God, and he will draw nigh to you (James 4: 7-8a KJV). Speaking of the blessings recorded in the first Psalm directly lead into the next chapter, entitled, **<u>Helpful Hints on How to be Blessed By God. You don't want to miss this chapter.</u>** There's one last gold nugget of advice that I want the readers to meditate on.

To defeat the Devil, do not concentrate on the negative events occurring in your lives. Rather, concentrate on the positive events. For example: let's say that you are the parents of six children. Four of the children are doing excellent in life.

Yet one or even two of them are having problems with the law, unemployment, drugs, or just acting foolish. Do your best to help the ones having trouble, but don't let the negative events of the two children; out weigh the positive events of the other four. In fact, spend the majority of the time meditating on the accomplishments of the other four.

This small act of change will give you a new outlook on life. A favorite song says, "I had some good days. I had some hills to climb. I had some weary days and I had some sleepless nights. But when I look around and think things over, all of my good days, out weigh my bad days and I can't complain. I can't complain because God has been good to me. Although my weary eyes can not see, but I'll say, thank you Lord. I can't complain."

Before moving on to the next chapter, write down at least three tidbits of information learned from the above chapter.

Dr. Stephen S. Lomax

1._____

2._____

3._____

CHAPTER XI

HELPFUL HINTS ON HOW TO BE BLESSED BY GOD!

"OBEDIENCE IS BETTER THAN SACRIFICE!"
"WHEN PRAISES GO UP; BLESSINGS COME DOWN!"

"If you will only obey the LORD your God, by diligently observing all his commandments that I am commanding you today, the LORD your God will set you high above all the nations of the earth; all these blessings shall come upon you and overtake you, if you obey the LORD your God:

Blessed shall you be in the city, and blessed shall you be in the field. Blessed shall be the fruit of your womb, the fruit of your ground, and the fruit of your livestock, both the increase of your cattle and the issue of your flock. Blessed shall be your basket and your kneading bowl.

Blessed shall you be when you come in, and blessed shall you be when you go out. The LORD will cause your enemies who rise against you to be defeated before you; they shall come out against you one way, and flee before you seven ways. The LORD will command the blessing upon you in your barns, and in all that you undertake; he will bless you in the land that the LORD your God is giving you.

The LORD will establish you as his holy people, as he has sworn to you, if you keep the commandments of the LORD your God and walk in his ways. All the peoples of the earth shall see that you are called by the name of the LORD, and they shall be afraid of you. The LORD will make you abound in prosperity, in the fruit of your womb, in the fruit of your livestock, and in the fruit of your ground in the land that the LORD swore to your ancestors to give you.

The LORD will open for you his rich storehouse, the heavens, to give the rain of your land in its season and to bless all your undertakings. You will lend to many nations, but you will not borrow. The LORD will make you the head, and not the tail; you shall be only at the top, and not at the bottom--if you obey the commandments of the LORD your God, which I am commanding you today, by diligently observing them, and if you do not turn aside from any of the words that I am commanding you today, either to the right or to the left, following other gods to serve them.

But if you will not obey the LORD your God by diligently observing all his commandments and decrees, which I am commanding you today, then all these curses shall come upon you and overtake you" (Deut. 28: 1-15 NRSV).

"Blessed is the man who does not walk in the counsel of the wicked or stand in the way of sinners or sit in the seat of mockers. But his delight is in the law of the LORD, and on his law he meditates day and night. He is like a tree planted by streams of water, which yields its fruit in season and whose leaf does not wither. Whatever he does prospers.

Not so the wicked! They are like chaff that the wind blows away. Therefore the wicked will not stand in the judgment, nor sinners in the assembly of the righteous. For the LORD watches over the way of the righteous, but the way of the wicked will perish" (I Psalm NIV).

"Isaac planted crops in that land and the same year reaped a hundredfold, because the LORD blessed him" (Genesis 26: 12 NIV).

"Bring the whole tithe into the storehouse, that there may be food in my house. Test me in this," says the LORD Almighty, "and see if I will not throw open the floodgates of heaven and pour out so much blessing that you will not have room enough for it.

I will prevent pests from devouring your crops, and the vines in your fields will not cast their fruit," says the LORD Almighty. "Then all the nations will call you blessed, for yours will be a delightful land," says the LORD Almighty" (Mal. 3: 10-12 NIV).

"For I am the LORD, I change not; therefore ye sons of Jacob are not consumed" (Mal. 3: 6 KJV). Jesus Christ the same yesterday, and to day, and for ever" (Hebrews 13: 8 KJV).

Somebody said, "Experience is the best teacher" and history is the best gage for determining the future." It is also said that history will repeat itself. The basic ideology is that history repeats itself because it lies in the hands of the God of repetition. God repeats Himself because he is a changeless God. The theologues (experts of theology) call this changelessness of God, immutability.

A more refined definition of "the immutability of God" is that He does not and can not change in essence because He operates in complete knowledge. "In countless passages of Scripture, the immutability of God is clearly taught. For example, in Malachi 3:6 God affirms, "I the Lord do not change." (See also Numbers 23:19; 1 Samuel 15:29; Isaiah 46:9-11; Ezekiel 24:14.)

James 1:17 tells us "Every good gift and every perfect gift is from above and comes down from the Father of lights, with whom is no variableness nor shadow of turning." The shadow of turning refers to the sun which eclipses, and turns, and casts its shadow. It rises and sets, appears and disappears every day; and it comes out of one tropic, and enters into another at certain seasons of the year.

But with God, who is light Himself, there is no darkness at all; there is no change, nor anything like it. He is unchangeable in His nature, perfections, purposes, promises, and gifts. He being holy; cannot turn to that which is evil; nor can He, who is the fountain of light, be the cause of darkness.

And since every good and perfect gift comes from Him, evil cannot proceed from him, nor can he tempt any to do it. The Bible is very clear that God does not change; neither, His mind, will, nor His nature:"[34]

Although it may appear that He does change. The apparent change may have been in the original plan of God all along, but only God knows for sure. For instance, when God sent Jonah to Nineveh, He told Jonah to tell the Ninevites that the city would be destroyed in forty days and forty nights.

Yet, once Jonah arrived and preached the message of doom and the people repented and returned to God, He forgave them and did not destroy the city. On the outside looking in, it could appear that God changed his mind. But, make note that goal of repentance was achieved, which was God's original purpose.

Additionally, don't forget that God created evil for man to have a choice. God has no part in evil or in evil temptations. Once again, it is the devil that "is going to and fro and up and down in the earth, seeking whom that he may devour."

Be reminded that we are God's prize creation; created just a little lower than the angels and the Devil will try to destroy us, even as early as in our mother's womb. Also remember that God wants us to overcome, while the devil wants us to fall and fail. The devil tempts us to bring us down, but God tests us to bring us up. It doesn't matter how dark the situation that we are in, God is the only light that will see us through. The reason is; he does not change and his word does not change. What He tells us today, He will stand on it tomorrow. Our responsibility is to be obedient to the word, if we are to be blessed by God.

Having stated that, the logic behind the immutability of God, suggests that the most helpful hints on the blessings of God are revealed in the examination of the blessed people of the past. In other words, since God does not change, it's reasonable to assume that what He did yesterday, He will do today.

The old preachers used to say that what He did for others, under similar circumstances, He will do the same for us. Therefore, it is a safe assumption that how He blessed those in the past, those in the present and in the future will be blessed the same.

To discover how to be blessed by God, the most logical place to begin is with those that were blessed in the past. The thought of that discussion for me centers around; Abraham. Out of all of the people of history that were blessed, the first name that comes to my mind is Abraham.

Likewise, when I think of patience, out of all of the people of history, Job comes to mind. When I think of strength, Sampson comes to mind: courage, David and Elijah; leadership, Moses and Joshua; temperament, Peter; loving, John and the list, go on and on.

On the other hand, when I think of cowardness; Barak comes to mind. Remember he would not fight without Deborah at his side. When I think of trickery, Jacob; drunkenness, Noah; Liar, Isaac; betrayer; Judas Iscariot; denier, Peter; hen pecked, King Ahab; romantic betrayal, Delilah; foolish for love, Sampson; etc.

But, in terms of the most blessed, Abraham was "the man." The Bible says, "And he blessed Abram, saying, "Blessed be Abram by God Most High, Creator of heaven and earth. And blessed be God Most High, who delivered your enemies into your hand." Then Abram gave him a tenth of everything" (Genesis 14: 19-20 NIV).

Again, the most logical person to begin a dialogue on blessedness is Abraham. Following the same line of thought, the first logical question to ask is; why did God bless him and in particular; bless him to become the father of the nations? The examination will begin with the books cited above, where the requirements for blessings are laid out by God.

From my experience, the first observation on how to be blessed is centered on the pleasing of the giver. It should be the goal of every receiver to please the giver. Wisdom suggests that the more the giver is pleased, the more the receiver will receive. This concept is not new. It has been around as long as man himself. In fact, it is seen in the Garden of Eden with Adam and Eve.

One theological perspective is that this concept played a starring role in the "Fall of Man." It has been suggested that Adam's participation in the eating of the forbidden fruit was motivated by a desire to please Mrs. Eve.

The Bibles says, "When the woman saw that the fruit of the tree was good for food and pleasing to the eye, and also desirable for gaining wisdom, she took some and ate it. She also gave some to her husband, who was with her, and he ate it" (Gen 3: 6 NIV).

It needs noting that Adam was created before Eve. In fact, she was created from a rib of Adam's side. The point being made here is that the serpent, no doubt, tried his trickery on Adam in some manner; in order to persuade him into disobedience and sin. Yet Adam did not yield to the serpent's enticement, but to Eve's.

Furthermore, the point is highlighted by Paul in the New Testament. He said, "For Adam was first formed, then Eve. And Adam was not deceived, but the woman being deceived was in the transgression" (I Tim 2:14 KJV). Of course Adam sinned, but he did so, trying to please the woman for a reward or gift: As man still does today. I am just pointing out the facts as I tell the story.

In the relationship of God and man, the situation is critically similar. As previously suggested, the goal of every receiver should be to please the giver. Thus, the first requirement of necessity in pleasing God (our Giver) is Faith. Let it be known that God is our Giver. In the great passage of John 3: 16, he notes, that "God so loved the world that He gave His only begotten Son that whosoever believeth in Him should not perish, but have everlasting life" (John 3: 16 KJV).

Also, know that to please God; **first,** we must have **faith.** The Scriptures are clear on this point as well. Paul said, "But without faith it is impossible to please him: for he that cometh to God must believe that he is, and that he is a rewarder of them that diligently seek him" (Hebrews 11: 6 KJV).

With faith also comes the requirement of fear and respect. Faith in the legislative power of the law maker; fear that the law maker will enforce the consequences of breaking the law and respect for the law maker, in terms of honor and justice (that the law maker will do the right thing). We have to have enough faith to know that if we disobey God's commandments, there will be consequences. But we must have enough respect for God to know that He will take care of his own.

In the text of Deuteronomy 28; all three requirements and the blessings are laid out. First the requirements: Again, God said, "If you will only obey the LORD your God, by diligently observing all his commandments that I am commanding you today, the LORD your God will set you high above all the nations of the earth" (Deut. 28: 1 NRSV).

The first requirement of obedience: we must have faith in the legislative power of the law giver. It doesn't matter what the circumstance. If there is no faith in the power of the legislature to enforce the rules that are enacted, there will be no obedience. For example: In driving the automobile on the highway and the legislature has enacted the speed limit of sixty five, but if there no police there with authority to enforce the speed limit, people will speed until "the cows come home."

In the home, the parent establishes all of the rules and regulations, but if there is no power or authority to enforce, the children will run wild through out the house. The list of examples, if written would be more than a mile long.

However, the point is this; when people believe in God and acknowledge his power to enforce the punishment for disobedience, there is greater attempt to obey. **The first requirement of obedience:** we must have fear that the law maker will enforce the consequences of breaking the law.

Parents have the power and authority to enforce, but some will not do so. By not doing so, they will never create fear in the children and thus will not receive obedience. This is seen on a regular basis. Parents have the God given right and authority "Train a child in the way he should go, and when he is old he will not turn from it" (Prov. 22: 6 NIV). Yet, they holler, yell and threaten the children with no response from the child.

On the other hand, there are parents that do not have to repeat their intention to the child and speak only once. The difference between the two: lies in the child's level of fear of the parent. One threat with no follow up and the other promises and keeps them.

In like manner, people that know God; fear him. In fact, the Scripture says, "The fear of the LORD is the beginning of knowledge: but fools despise wisdom and instruction" (Prov. 1: 7 KJV). Jesus said, "And fear not them which kill the body, but are not able to kill the soul: but rather fear him which is able to destroy both soul and body in hell" (Matt. 10: 28 NRSV).

Although some may disagree that the child should fear the parent, but I say, some fear of authority can be a good thing. **The second requirement of obedience:** we must respect the law maker, in terms of honor and justice; knowing that he will do the right thing. Micah asked, "Wherewith shall I come before the LORD, and bow myself before the high God? Shall I come before him with burnt offerings, with calves of a year old?

Will the LORD be pleased with thousands of rams, or with ten thousands of rivers of oil? Shall I give my firstborn for my transgression, the fruit of my body for the sin of my soul?

He hath showed thee, O man, what is good; and what doth the LORD require of thee, but to do justly, and to love mercy, and to walk humbly with thy God" (Micah 6: 6-8 KJV)?

God said to Amos, go and tell the people, "I hate, I despise your feast days, and I will not smell in your solemn assemblies. Though ye offer me burnt offerings and your meat offerings, I will not accept them: neither will I regard the peace offerings of your fat beasts. Take thou away from me the noise of thy songs; for I will not hear the melody of thy viols. But let judgment run down as waters, and righteousness as a mighty stream "(Amos 5: 21-24 KJV).

God is a good God. We can trust and depend upon him to do the right thing. The old preachers used to say, God is too good to do wrong, too wise to make any mistakes and too strong to come up short. Besides, obedience is better than sacrifice.

The Bible says, "Hath the LORD as great delight in burnt offerings and sacrifices, as in obeying the voice of the LORD? Behold, to obey is better than sacrifice, and to hearken than the fat of rams" (I Sam. 15: 22 KJV).

If through faith, fear and respect; we obey God; He will bless. The Bible says, "**The Lord your God will set you high above all the nations**

of the earth; all these blessings shall come upon you and overtake you" (Deut. 28: 1 KJV). In the great temptation of Jesus at the River Jordan, Satan offered Jesus the same blessings that are being offered here by God (Matt 4:)

However, there is a difference; when God gives, the gifts are permanent. When Satan gives, the gifts are temporary. Satan is an Indian giver. But not only are the gifts temporary from Satan, they are given as an enticement for evil. Satan gives gifts to set men and women up for a fall. Be careful at the reception of gifts from evil people or the Evil One. Don't accept anything that you can not afford to lose. Neither, allow the Devil to bribe you.

On the other hand, it's good to know that God doesn't set people up or bribe them. His gifts are given honestly and sincerely. Moses said, "If we obey God, He will bless. "Blessed shall you be in the city, and blessed shall you be in the field.

Blessed shall be the fruit of your womb, the fruit of your ground, and the fruit of your livestock, both the increase of your cattle and the issue of your flock. Blessed shall be your basket and your kneading bowl. Blessed shall you be when you come in, and blessed shall you be when you go out" (Deut. 28: 2-6 NRSV).

The songwriter said, "You can't beat God giving, no matter how hard you try." Those of us that know, "you can't beat God giving," aim high and expect to succeed. We place ourselves in the pathway of blessings. We make ourselves available for the touch of God.

Even though there is not a Biblical passage that states it, nonetheless, it is true: "If we make one step, God will make two." "If we do our part; God will do his." God said to Solomon, "If my people which are called by my name shall humble themselves and pray, seek my face, turn from their wicked ways; then I will hear from heaven and forgive their sins and heal their land" (II Chron. 7: 14 KJV).

But before moving on to the issue of blessings, there's a more urgent question for the reader: where do you stand in belief and acknowledgement of God? Do you really believe in Him? Are your actions a testimony of your beliefs?

To help you arrive at the destination of obedience, again allow me to make a few suggestions. The first one is to read and study your Bibles daily. The second one is to establish regular prayer routines. Third one is to step out on faith, in response to God's commands. It's been said, "It's better to have tried and failed; than to never have tried at all." Also, it is said, "When at first you don't succeed, try and try again."

In the book of Malachi, chapter, 3: 10, God asked man to try Him. God said, "Bring the full tithe into the storehouse, so that there may be food in my house, (try me) **and thus, put me to the test,** says the LORD of hosts; see if I will not open the windows of heaven for you and pour down for you an overflowing blessing.

I will rebuke the locust for you, so that it will not destroy the produce of your soil; and your vine in the field shall not be barren, says the LORD of hosts. Then all nations will count you happy, for you will be a land of delight, says the LORD of hosts" (Mal. 3: 10-12 NRSV).

Just in case, there is someone reading this book that feels like, they do not deserve the blessings of God. Maybe you have done much wrong and have committed much evil and have assessed yourself unworthy of God's goodness. But, before you give up on God and yourself; please take the time to read the remainer of this chapter and the book as a whole.

The Apostle Paul's life is a testimony to the wicked or the un-churched repenting and turning from their wicked ways to the blessings of God. Briefly, in Paul's own words, the story goes like this: "I persecuted the followers of this Way to their death, arresting both men and women and throwing them into prison, as also the high priest and all the Council can testify.

I even obtained letters from them to their brothers in Damascus, and went there to bring these people as prisoners to Jerusalem to be punished. About noon as I came near Damascus, suddenly a bright light from heaven flashed around me. I fell to the ground and heard a voice say to me, 'Saul! Saul! Why do you persecute me?' Who are you, Lord?' I asked. I am Jesus of Nazareth, whom you are persecuting,' he replied.

My companions saw the light, but they did not understand the voice of him who was speaking to me. What shall I do, Lord? I asked. Get up, the Lord said, and go into Damascus. There you will be told all that you have been assigned to do. My companions led me by the hand into Damascus, because the brilliance of the light had blinded me.

A man named Ananias came to see me. He was a devout observer of the law and highly respected by all the Jews living there. He stood beside me and said, 'Brother Saul, receive your sight!' And at that very moment I was able to see him. Then he said: 'The God of our fathers has chosen you to know his will and to see the Righteous One and to hear words from his mouth" (Acts 22: 4-14 NIV).

The message is clear. It does not matter what an individual has done, if he is willing to turn from the wickedness, God will forgive and give him another chance to be blessed. As stated above, Paul persecuted the Church to the fullest, killing holy men and women, yet God forgave him and blessed his life.

He was blessed to the point that in his last breath, Paul said, "I have fought the good fight, I have finished the race, I have kept the faith. Now there is in store for me the crown of righteousness, which the Lord, the righteous Judge, will award to me on that day--and not only to me, but also to all who have longed for his appearing" (I Tim. 4: 7-8 NIV).

Finally also, I am a living witness to the blessings of God as a result of repentance and obedience. I am the youngest of nine children raised by a hard working, single mother. You know much about my childhood all ready; yet, God blessed me to graduate from North Greenville College with an Associate of Arts degree.

He blessed me to graduate form the University of South Carolina at Spartanburg with a Bachelors of Arts degree. He blessed me to graduate from the Erskine College with a Master of Divinity degree. He blessed me to graduate from the Erskine Seminary with a Doctor of ministry degree.

God has blessed me with great health and strength. He has blessed my family as well: my lovely wife, three daughters and a son along with the son in laws and the two grandchildren. He has blessed my ministry, although I have had my share of ups and downs as all ministers.

At present, He is blessing the New Life in Christ Missionary Baptist Church of Fountain Inn, S. C. where I am the organizer and pastor. He has blessed me to write this book and share these Biblical truths with the readers on "How to be blessed by God."

The final analysis of it all is to understand the necessity of making certain changes in your life. After which, step out on faith, position yourselves in the blessing line and wait to be blessed. For God is good all of the time and all of the time, God is good and He loves blessing His children.

Since the chapter began with Abraham, his life is good place to end. Abraham followed the instructions that are being suggested in the book. When God called him to go to a place that he was unfamiliar, he went. When God asked him to step out on faith, he did.

Not only did he go to a place of unfamiliarity, but He took his son to Mount Moriah to offer him there as a sacrifice. He positioned himself in the valley of blessings. Abraham did his part and waited on God to do his. The Biblical report is that time and time a gain, God showed up and showed out.

Remember, what God did for others, He will do for you and me today. So cheer up my brothers and sisters; God is on our side. Know that, "if God be for us; He is more than the whole world against us." The Apostle Paul said it this way, "I can do all things through Christ which strengtheneth me" (Phil. 4: 13, KJV).

The angel of the Lord said to Mary, "And, behold, thy cousin Elisabeth, she hath also conceived a son in her old age: and this is the sixth month with her, who was called barren. For with God nothing shall be impossible" (Luke 1: 36-37 KJV). Let us remember the awesome power of God as we move on to the final chapter and write down at least three tidbits of information learned from the above chapter.

1._____

2._____

3._____

CHAPTER XII

A FINAL THOUGHT!

IF YOU DON'T KNOW WHO YOU'RE MESSING WITH, YOU NEED TO ASK SOMEBODY!

"Then some itinerant Jewish exorcists tried to use the name of the Lord Jesus over those who had evil spirits, saying, "I adjure you by the Jesus whom Paul proclaims." Seven sons of a Jewish high priest named Sceva were doing this. But the evil spirit said to them in reply, "Jesus I know, and Paul I know; but who are you?"

Then the man with the evil spirit leaped on them, mastered them all, and so overpowered them that they fled out of the house naked and wounded. When this became known to all residents of Ephesus, both Jews and Greeks, everyone was awestruck; and the name of the Lord Jesus was praised. Also many of those who became believers confessed and disclosed their practices." (Acts 19: 14-18 NRSV).

In the final thought on the book, the above theme suggests three perspectives that I want to leave with the readers for consideration. The first one is addressed to the Christian, if you don't know much about the Devil, you need to ask somebody. The second one is addressed to the world, if you don't know much about the Christian, you need to ask somebody.

The third one is addressed to the Christian Church, if you don't know much about yourselves, in terms of who you are; you need to ask somebody. For the church's ignorance of these facts is killing the effectiveness of the church's ministry in the world.

The church's ignorance of these facts is a reminder of a situation that occurred when I was young man. As stated periodically throughout the book, I grew up in a community called Green Line. During my youth, Green Line was considered a rough and tough community (as many other communities were at the time).

Allow me a moment to interrupt the story and tell you that my experiences living in the hood were not easy and were the reasons that at my first opportunity, I moved to the suburbs. Also the constant threats of violence and the peer pressure of criminal activity added to my exodus: along with the fact that I did not want my children to face the kinds of decisions that I did on a daily basis.

Although, many have said that I turned out all right, I say, "But by the grace of God I am what I am: and his grace which was bestowed upon me was not in vain" (I Cor. 15: 10a NIV): A few facts for parents to consider, who have the option of relocation.

Having said that; let me finish the story. One of the other rival communities (at least considered that way by the young in the neighborhood) was named Field Crest. In the seventh grade, I had to attend High School at Beck High School which was in the Field Crest Community.

I will never forget the first day I arrived at the high school, a young man who will remain unnamed, met me as I was stepping off of the bus. He was a member of a rival group and the first words out his mouth were; "Do you want to box me?"

Quite honestly, I really did not, but felt like I had no choice. (There it is again, peer pressure.) Yet I agreed because the Green Line community needed to represent (as the young folk said). As the boxing match proceeded, I was doing better than expected.

In fact, I was representing pretty well, bobbing and weaving and the like. That is, until somewhere between bob and weave, he kicked me above the right eye.

According to the rules, this was a dirty and low down move on his part, since we are boxing with only the use of our hands. At this change in the rules, I had no choice (if I was going compete and represent) but to adapt to the new rule: which was, there were no rules and anything goes. As Malcolm X used to say; "By any means necessary."

Unfortunately, most of the memories of my life included violence. By the citing of many of them does not in any way mean that I am advocating violence: I am not. As followers of Christ, we know that we are to "love our enemies, bless them that curse us, do good to them that hate us and pray for them which despitefully use and persecute us" (Matt. 5: 44 KJV).

It just so happened that violence was the reality of growing up in a rough and tough community. The only reason for citing the above example was to make this point. The church (the Body of Jesus Christ) must adapt its fight to the level of the competition of the Devil. The church is trying to fight, following the rules and regulations suggested by the Devil.

Yet, the Devil is fighting without following any rules. More specifically, the Devil has no rules. He is as low down and dirty as they come. On top of all that, he has no remorse for anything down and dirty that he does.

In a wrestling match, the Devil kicks, scratches, punches, even cuts and shoots, knowing; he's violating every rule in the book. As a young man, out of all of the violence I experienced; I learned one thing, you can't win, fighting the enemy's fight and on his territory.

If there will be victory, it will be achieved by fighting the right fight. The Bible says, "Fight the good fight of faith" (I Tim. 6: 12 KJV). Paul said, "So fight I, not as one that beateth the air" (I Cor. 9: 26 KJV).

His final address was to Timothy was, "I have fought a good fight, I have finished my course, I have kept the faith: Henceforth there is laid up for me a crown of righteousness, which the Lord, the righteous judge, shall give me at that day: and not to me only, but unto all them also that love his appearing" (I Tim. 4: 7-8 KJV).

In order for the church to achieve victory, it is going to have to adapt to the fight of the Devil. The church must construct strategies that play to its strengths; not weaknesses. The first thing necessary for the church to achieve victory is to get serious and get real. It's going to have to realize that there is a war going on.

By the preponderance of Scripture already presented, it should be crystal clear that the Devil is not playing games with you and me and nobody else. He is trying with all of his might and knowledge to knock our heads right off of our shoulders. As one of my coaches used to say, "We need to get our heads in the game."

To accomplish getting our heads in the game, we need to examine the three perspectives presented in Acts 19. Once again, the first one is addressed to the Christian; if you don't know much about the Devil, you need to ask somebody. The second one is addressed to the world, if you don't know much about the Christian, you need to ask somebody.

The third one is addressed to the Christian Church, if you don't know much about yourselves, in terms of who you are; you need to ask somebody. **In response to the first perspective** about the Devil, it needs noting that Paul knew much about the Devil and his demons.

In fact, (like Jesus in Mark 5 and so many other passages of Scripture), Paul was having his way with the demons in Ephesus. The Bible says, he (Paul) had been there two years and God worked great miracles by his hands (Acts 19: 11). "So much so that even handkerchiefs and aprons that had touched him were taken to the sick, and their illnesses were cured and the evil spirits left them" (Acts 19: 12 NIV).

Paul knew that the Devil was real and cunning. He knew that the Devil was a serious threat to mankind's existence. He warned mankind, he said, "Finally, be strong in the Lord and in his mighty power. Put on the full armor of God so that you can take your stand against the devil's schemes.

For our struggle is not against flesh and blood, but against the rulers, against the authorities, against the powers of this dark world and against the spiritual forces of evil in the heavenly realms. Therefore put on the full armor of God, so that when the day of evil comes, you may be able to stand your ground, and after you have done everything, to stand.

Stand firm then, with the belt of truth buckled around your waist, with the breastplate of righteousness in place, and with your feet fitted with the readiness that comes from the gospel of peace. In addition to all this, take up the shield of faith, with which you can extinguish all the flaming arrows of the evil one.

Take the helmet of salvation and the sword of the Spirit, which is the word of God. And pray in the Spirit on all occasions with all kinds of prayers and requests. With this in mind, be alert and always keep on praying for all the saints" (Eph. 6: 10-18 NIV).

So when the church recognizes the existence of the Devil and exercises its power over him and put him back into his place, there is no force on the earth that can hinder her progress. However, in response to **the second perspective,** the Bible says, "there were some Jews who went around driving out evil spirits, and they tried to invoke the name of the Lord Jesus over those who were demon-possessed. They would say, "In the name of Jesus, whom Paul preaches, I command you to come out.

They are identified as "the seven sons of Sceva, a Jewish chief priest, were doing this. One day the evil spirit answered them, "Jesus I know, and I know about Paul, but who are you?" Then the man who had the evil spirit jumped on them and overpowered them all. He gave them such a beating that they ran out of the house naked and bleeding" (Acts 19: 12-16 NIV).

Apparently these seven sons did not know the capability of the Devil and his demons. The Devil has power and is mean and evil. The seven son's ignorance almost cost them their lives. The church's ignorance of the Devil and his capabilities cost us greatly today.

It has been repeatedly quoted that if you think education cost, try ignorance: particularly ignorance of the Devil. Man needs to know that the Devil is a destroyer and is going to and fro in the earth seeking whom he may devour" (I Peter 5: 8 KJV).

To the world, the text further addresses the second perspective: **If you don't know who the Christian is, you need to ask somebody.** The Christian has power. It has been repeatedly demonstrated in Scripture that the Christian is somebody to be reckoned with; when he is in connection with God.

In this text, the demons recognized the power of the Christian. The evil spirit said, "Jesus I know and Paul I know." They were respectful, even obedient to both Jesus and Paul. The demoniac (known as legion) of Mark five was fearfully, respectful as well.

Accordingly, today, the demonic presence will respect, honor and obey the Christian. Therefore, it would be in the best interest of the world to acknowledge the power and the connection of God to the Christian.

There is danger to the world for failure to recognize the difference between the Christian and the non-Christian. The seven sons of Sceva (Non-Christian, remember the evil declared that he knew them not) tried to exercise the power of the Christian.

Yet, the Devil and his demons did not respect, honor or obey the son's requests; rather the evil spirit was angered by their pretense and responded with a beat down.

In actuality the Bible says, the evil spirit reacted with the words, "Jesus I know, and Paul I know, but who are you?" Then the man who had the evil spirit jumped on them and overpowered them all. He gave them such a beating that they ran out of the house naked and bleeding" (Acts 19: 12-16 NIV).

Finally, **the third and last perspective** in the text is addressed to the Christian Church: **"If you don't know much about yourselves, in terms of who you are; you need to ask somebody.** If indeed the individual Christian has power and authority, so much more does the Christian Church. Jesus replied to Peter, "Blessed are you, Simon son of Jonah, for this was not revealed to you by man, but by my Father in heaven.

And I tell you that you are Peter, and on this rock I will build my church, and the gates of Hades will not overcome it. I will give you the keys of the kingdom of heaven; whatever you bind on earth will be bound in heaven, and whatever you loose on earth will be loosed in heaven" (Matt. 16: 17-19 NIV). The Christian Church has power because of the name, Jesus.

Here is another example to consider. Once again, on Green Line, there was bully, whose name will remain anonymous. I was in the first or second grade. He was in the third grade and bullied me for the first few days of the school year. I have already mentioned that I was the youngest of nine children, six boys and three girls.

The brother that was next to me was a year or so older. He was the same age of the bully that was bothering me. One day, he heard that I was being bullied by the person whose name I will not call. Although, it was nearly fifty years ago, obviously, you know that I remember his name. I remember it because it was a very traumatic time in my life.

But one day, my brother told me not to run from _____, he would be in the bushes when he approaches me and he will handle it. The only thing that I had to do was trust him and not run.

The bully, _____ ran up and tried to bully me. My brother jumped out the bushes and clocked him good, one for the Father, one for the Son and one for the Holy Ghost. I'm just joking, but he did clock him good and he ran off. The bully never bothered me again.

The reason I tell you the story is to encourage the Christian. As a Lomax; I had a big brother. In fact, I had five big brothers and all I had to do was let any one of them know that I was having trouble. I suffered the bullying for days, un-necessarily. Once I knew who I was (somebody with a big brother) and the bully knew who I was, my life improved immeasurably.

The Christian and the Christian Church needs to realize who they are and to whom, they belong. Christians needs to realize that they belong to the family of God and they too have a big brother. His name is Jesus. The Bible said, "There came then his brethren and his mother, and, standing without, sent unto him, calling him.

And the multitude sat about him, and they said unto him, Behold, thy mother and thy brethren without seek for thee. And he answered them, saying, Who is my mother, or my brethren? And he looked round about on them which sat about him, and said, Behold my mother and my brethren! For whosoever shall do the will of God, the same is my brother, and my sister, and mother" (Mark 3: 31 -35 KJV).

The Church need not to be afraid of the bully named Satan, The Bible says, "Trust in the Lord and lean not to your own understanding, in all thy ways acknowledge him and he shall direct they path" (Proverbs 3: 5-6 KJV). The Christian is somebody and need to know that they have power and authority because of their big brother. In fact, the church as a whole need to realize its blood line and take back its proper place of preeminence in the world.

Yet, there is a reason that the church has lost its place in the world and evil people don't respect the church. There is a reason that the evil spirits don't respect the church. In fact, there is a reason that evil in general don't respect the church.

The reason is obvious; the Christian Church doesn't respect itself. There are many churches just as guilty of immorality as the world is. There is smoking, drinking, cussing, fighting, lying, gossiping, backbiting, envy, jealousy, fornication, adultery, evil conspiracies of all kinds; right on the church's grounds and sometimes even inside of the church's buildings.

There are many people that either don't know (through plain ignorance of the Scripture) or have forgotten (through bad memories) the warnings of God about the Holy ground. In a conversation with Moses, the Bible said, "There the angel of the LORD appeared to him in a flame of fire out of a bush; he looked, and the bush was blazing, yet it was not consumed. Then Moses said, "I must turn aside and look at this great sight, and see why the bush is not burned up.

When the LORD saw that he had turned aside to see, God called to him out of the bush, "Moses, Moses!" And he said, "Here I am. **Then he said, "Come no closer! Remove the sandals from your feet, for the place on which you are standing is holy ground"** (Exo. 3: 5 NRSV).

If the church is serious about defeating the devil and engaging in effective ministry to the lost, it must re-examine and re-commit itself. If the church wants respect and involvement from the world, it must begin to respect it self. The great commission has never been more necessary than today. But first, the church must heed its own message before it can take it to the world.

Surely, there will be opposition; we should know by now that the Devil is skilled at his job. But the church must not allow him to hinder the work of the kingdom. There is too much at stake. This is a war that mankind can not afford to lose. The eternal souls of too many people are at risk. Don't concentrate on the opposers; but on the supporters.

Even at the mountain in Galilee; to Jesus' last command to the church, there was opposition. The Bible says, "Now the eleven disciples went to Galilee, to the mountain to which Jesus had directed them. When they saw him, they worshiped him; **but some doubted" (Matt. 28: 16-17 NRSV). Remember the four D's of the Devil: Desire, doubt, deception and disobedience.**

As long as there is a Devil in the world, there will be opposition to the work of God. Don't get discouraged, Paul said, "Do not be overcome by evil, but **overcome** evil with good" (Romans 12: 21 NRSV). I write to you, young people, because you are strong and the word of God abides in you, and you have **overcome** the evil one" (I John 2: 14b NRSV).

What about the words of Jesus in the real Lord's Prayer? He said, "These things I have spoken unto you, that in me ye might have peace. In the world ye shall have tribulation: but be of good cheer; I have **overcome** the world" (John 16: 33 KJV).

Finally, "Jesus came and said to them, "All authority in heaven and on earth has been given to me. Go therefore and make disciples of all nations, baptizing them in the name of the Father and of the Son and of the Holy Spirit, and teaching them to obey everything that I have commanded you. And remember, I am with you always, to the end of the age. Amen and Amen, again" (Matt. 28: 18-20 NRSV).

Here's something to remember, "When your memories are bigger than your dreams, you are moving in the wrong direction." Solomon asked the question, what is the conclusion of the matter? The conclusion is this: I thank you for your consideration of the facts as presented to you.

Although I don't know you, I am concerned about your soul. Therefore as a favor to me, please examine your salvation. Knowing what you do now about the realities of the Devil; are you positive that you are saved? The Devil is real and you don't want to spend eternity in his midst, so have you repented and turned from following him to Jesus Christ our Lord?

If you are wondering, how do I accept Jesus Christ? Repeat and answer the following: Do you believe in Jesus Christ? Do you believe that He is God's Son; born of a virgin named Mary? Do you believe that He died on a rugged cross for the sins of the world, including your sins? Do you believe that on the third day, God raised him from the dead?

If you repented and believe what you just read, you are saved. Romans 10: 9 says, "That if thou shalt confess with thy mouth the Lord Jesus, and shalt believe in thine heart that God hath raised him from the dead, thou shalt be saved. For with the heart man believeth unto righteousness; and with the mouth confession is made unto salvation. For the scripture saith; whosoever believeth on him shall not be ashamed" (Romans 10: 9-11 KJV).

The final act of the book, write down at least three tidbits of information learned from the above chapter.

1._____

2._____

3._____

Legend of Abbreviations for Books of the Bible

Old Testament Abbreviations

Gen.	Genesis	**2Chron.**	2 Chronicles	**Dan.**	Daniel
Ex.	Exodus	**Ezra**	Ezra	**Hos.**	Hosea
Lev.	Leviticus	**Neh.**	Nehemiah	**Joel**	Joel
Num.	Numbers	**Est.**	Esther	**Amos**	Amos
Deut.	Deuteronomy	**Job**	Job	**Obad.**	Obadiah
Josh.	Joshua	**Ps.**	Psalms	**Jonah**	Jonah
Judg.	Judges	**Prov.**	Proverbs	**Mic.**	Micah
Ruth	Ruth	**Eccles.**	Ecclesiastes	**Nah.**	Nahum
1 Sam.	1 Samuel	**Song**	Song of Solomon	**Hab.**	Habakkuk
2Sam.	2 Samuel	**Is.**	Isaiah	**Zeph.**	Zephaniah
1 Kings	1 Kings	**Jer.**	Jeremiah	**Hag.**	Haggai
2Kings	2 Kings	**Lam.**	Lamentations	**Zech.**	Zechariah
1 Chr.	1 Chronicles	**Ezek.**	Ezekiel	**Mal.**	Malachi

New Testament Abbreviations

Matt.	Matthew	**Eph.**	Ephesians	**Heb.**	Hebrews
Mk.	Mark	**Phil.**	Philippians	**Js.**	James
Lk.	Luke	**Col.**	Colossians	**1 Pet.**	1 Peter
Jn.	John	**1 Thess.**	1 Thessalonians	**2Pet.**	2 Peter
Acts	Acts	**2Thess.**	2 Thessalonians	**1 Jn.**	1 John
Rom.	Romans	**1 Tim.**	1 Timothy	**2Jn.**	2 John
1 Cor.	1 Corinthians	**2Tim.**	2 Timothy	**3Jn.**	3 John
2Cor.	2 Corinthians	**Tit.**	Titus	**Jude**	Jude
Gal.	Galatians	**Philem.**	Philemon	**Rev.**	Revelation

END NOTES ON BOOK:

1. Wikipedia Free Encyclopedia
2. New York Times, April 19, 2007
3. The Sudney Morning Herald
4. Bangkok Post
5. Bangkok Post
6. Webster's New Encyclopedia Dictionary
7. The Study of Ants, Longman, London; Sudd, J. H. 1967
8. The State of Man Before the Fall and the Covenant of Nature by Dr. Francis Turretin.
9. Time. Com/time/nation/article/0,8599,340694-3,00html
10. James H. Thom - Edythe Draper, Draper's Book of Quotations for the Christian
11. Karl Rahner, quoted in the Wittenburg Door (June/July 1988). Christianity Today, Vol. 34, no. 8.
12. The Biblical Illustrator; Baker, pg. 198
13. Varsity Bible Dictionary
14. Pictorial Biblical Dictionary, p. 215
15. Wikipedia, the free encyclopedia
16. Lincoln's children Zoo article
17. Flores, Fernando. Print publication date: 2003 Published to Oxford Scholarship Online: November 2003
18. Pictorial Biblical Dictionary, p. 215
19. American Educator **Winter 2002**
20. Wikipedia, the free encylopedia
21. The Twentieth Century New Testament; TCNT
22. Westminster Shorter Catechism, Q4

23. Pictorial Bible Dictionary, pg 316
24. A Catholic Understanding of the Story of Creation and the Fall
25. World (Wheaton: Tyndale House Publishers, Inc., 1992). Entry 3436.
26. What does it mean that we are created in God's image? By Marshall Beretta & Cathy Ramey
27. A Catholic Understanding of the Story of Creation and the Fall
28. Disturbed About Man; Dr. Benjamin E. Mayes
29. The Purpose Driven Life; Rick Warren
30. Contending For the Faith; Answers to the Bible, Vol I.
31. Theopedia: "Free Will!"
32. Cherbonnier; Human Nature
33. Frequently asked questions by Don Stewart
34. Answers for Atheist and Agnostics: Rich Deem.
35. Dwight Smith; the Renovation Center, 2008
36. Wikipedia, the free encylopedia
37. The Purpose Driven Life; Rick Warren.
38. Got Questions. Org "What is the immutability of God?
39. Pictorial Bible Dictionary, (pg. 575).

Printed in the United States
123154LV00004BA/154-435/P